A MONOGRAPH OF THE SILVER DOLLAR

A MONOGRAPH OF THE SILVER DOLLAR GOOD AND BAD

J. L. RIDDELL

Published by

FacsiMile Publisher
12 Pragati Market
Ashok Vihar, Ph-2
Delhi - 110052, India
Phone: 011-47034999
Email: www.facsimilepublishers.com
info@facsimilepublishers.com

Distribution Network
gyanbooks.com
India, USA, Canada, UK, Australia

ISBN: 978-93-6896-732-3 (PB)
First Published, 1845

2nd Impression 2025

Printed at: Gyan Press, Delhi.

A MONOGRAPH OF THE SILVER DOLLAR
Author: J. L. RIDDELL

A MONOGRAPH OF THE SILVER DOLLAR, GOOD AND BAD.

ILLUSTRATED WITH FAC-SIMILE FIGURES OF FOUR HUNDRED AND TWENTY-FIVE VARIETIES OF DOLLARS, AND EIGHTY-SEVEN VARIETIES OF HALF DOLLARS, INCLUDING THE GENUINE, THE LOW STANDARD, AND THE COUNTERFEIT: GIVING THEIR WEIGHT, QUALITY AND EXACT VALUE, AND ENABLING THE INEXPERIENCED TO DETECT THOSE WHICH ARE SPURIOUS.

BY J. L. RIDDELL, M. D.

MELTER AND REFINER IN THE UNITED STATES BRANCH MINT, NEW ORLEANS; AND PROFESSOR OF CHEMISTRY IN THE MEDICAL COLLEGE OF LOUISIANA.

THE ORIGINAL ASSAYS MADE BY WM. P. HORT, M. D., ASSAYER IN THE UNITED STATES BRANCH MINT, NEW ORLEANS.

NEW ORLEANS:
SOLD BY NORMAN, NEW ORLEANS; WILEY AND PUTNAM, NEW YORK; CAREY & HART, PHILADELPHIA; E. MORGAN & CO., CINCINNATI.

PRINTED BY E. SHEPARD, CINCINNATI.

1845.

ADVERTISEMENT.

The author would respectfully announce, that he has nearly prepared for publication "A General Atlas of Modern Coins," upon the plan of the present work. It will be fully illustrated by perfect fac-simile figures, and will, it is presumed, be found useful, not only in giving the authentic and exact quality and value of the multiform varieties of hard money, but also in affording valuable and ready means of distinguishing the genuine from the spurious.

Branch Mint, New Orleans,
August, 1845.

PRELIMINARY REMARKS,

ON THE DESCRIPTION, WEIGHT, VALUE AND IMPRESSION OF COINS, AND ON COUNTERFEITS.

I. Description of Coins.

In the description of coins, either side is called the *disc*.

The principal side, usually bearing a bust, portrait, or human figure, is denominated the *obverse*.

The other side, bearing usually a coat of arms or other characteristic insignia, is denominated the *reverse*.

Words, &c., running circularly near the margin or edge, are denominated the *legend*, as UNITED STATES OF AMERICA on the reverse of No. 3.

Words, &c., running in straight lines horizontally across the face, are denominated the *inscription*.

Words, figures, &c., running in a straight line horizontally near the bottom, are denominated the *exergue*.

The positions of parts of an object, are spoken of in reference to the object itself: thus in No. 3, the eagle holds arrows in his *dexter* or *right* claw, and an olive branch in his *sinister* or *left* claw.

II. Explanation of the Ways in which the Weights of the Coins are Expressed.

The weights of the genuine coins will be found expressed in reference to three different standards; dollars, grains and grammes.

1st. The Dollar of the United States as at present coined, (Vide No. 5,) is assumed as unity or 1, and any specific weight is decimally expressed, thus affording a direct and rational comparison of weight with our standard Dollar. By using a pair of common apothecary scales, and counterbalancing the coin with our dollars, dimes and half dimes, coined since 1838, a fair approximation towards the weight can, by any person, be made. Or in the absence of scales the following plan will answer :—Make a light rule of wood, say 8 inches long, 1 inch broad, and $\frac{1}{8}$ of an inch thick: balance it across the middle on the edge of a knife, and mark the centre of gravity:

measure each way from the centre, say 3½ inches, and mark the distance transversely across the rule. Lay the coin to be weighed centrally on one of these transverse marks, and add unworn American silver coins to counterbalance the same, in like manner to the other mark. For convenience, each end of the rule may rest on a block, so that a knife edge may be passed beneath the central line for poising. For weights smaller than $0.050, the half dime, or its equivalent weight in wire, may be subdivided into 5 equal parts, each equal to $0.010.

The standard American Dollar alluded to, weighs very nearly, if not worn, 412.5 grains, or 26.72 French grammes. In respect to counterfeits, I have stated the weight in the Dollar as an integer, without expressing the equivalency in grains and grammes.

The Dollar mark, when intended to imply weight, has a small ʷ affixed to it, thus : $ʷ.

III. Explanation of the Manner in which the Values of the Coins are Expressed.

The Dollar of the United States, assumed as the standard, weighing 412.5 grains, and containing 900 parts fine silver in 1000 parts, speaks for itself.

The English sovereign, of full legal weight (123¼ grs.) and fineness, (916⅔—1000ths), would be worth in American (U. S.) gold, between $4.86 and $4.87.

Gold is the legal tender in England for large amounts, and the chief material of hard money there. Twenty shillings of account make a sovereign or pound. The value of the Dollar expressed in these shillings of account would be near 4.1084*s.* or in shillings and pence and decimals of pence, 4*s.* 1.3*d.*

These shillings and pence, it must be borne in mind, refer to the legal sovereign or pound of twenty shillings of account, not to the actual shillings, &c., coined in the British Mint. The shilling of account is worth 24⅓ cts. of American (U. S.) silver, while the Victoria silver shilling is worth only 21⅔ cts.,=10.7*d.* making a difference of almost 11 per cent.

In point of fact, the gold of the English sovereign is only 915½—1000ths fine, and its real value is, therefore, near $4.85 when of full weight.

I have thought it advisable to express the value of the genuine coins in 1st, Dollars of the United States, and decimals. 2d, English shillings of account, pence and decimals of a penny, and 3d, in French francs and decimals or centimes, assuming the silver franc to be of full legal weight and fineness, and worth in our money, $0.187.

IV. Dies Used in Coining.

The only material possessing conjointly sufficient hardness, strength and tenacity, to impress any design successively upon a great number of pieces of gold or silver, is hardened steel. The design, in the first place, must have been either engraved in the steel, or communicated to it by impression from another previously engraved piece of steel, the latter hardened, the former, the receiving steel at the time, in an annealed or softened condition.

It is no small labor to engrave a steel die *de novo*, in a finished style, and with a complicated design; and it is perhaps unattainable by art to counterfeit perfectly, or in other words, to produce by engraving in steel, an exact fac-simile of such a die. Hence the security of well made dies, properly guarded, against the production of spurious money.

The following, at the present day, is the most approved method of preparing dies for coinage:—The artist, in the first place, engraves many of the objects to be represented on the coin upon distinct steel punches, such as the bust, figures, letters, and items that are repeated in the legend, coat of arms, &c. With these he proceeds to make female dies, similar to those used in coining, finishing the same, and adding thereto by engraving: a work altogether that for a single pair of dies, sometimes occupies many months. When completed, the steel is hardened, and thus is made a pair of *original dies*. The impressions are then communicated by great pressure, careful annealing, pressure again, the pressing and annealing being successively many times repeated, until the whole designs are perfectly transferred, resembling in steel the coins to be formed. Thus a pair of *king dies* is produced. Several pairs of king dies are thus formed, where an extensive coinage is contemplated. The letters and figures in relief are next ground over and polished; then the king dies are hardened, after which, in turn they are used precisely as described in reference to their own production, to form female or *working dies* to be used in stamping gold or silver. The impression in the female dies having been made perfect, a steel punch is used to add probably the last figure of the date, and another punch perhaps for a mint mark. The whole surface of the female dies is then ground very slightly convex and polished; after which they are hardened and again polished.

It may be inferred from their coins for the last forty years, that the French and English pursue the foregoing plan or others equally systematic. Those coins are very rarely counterfeited. The mint of the United States has also pursued a like regular system in the production of dies since the year 1836, although there have occasionally been changes in the original dies. It is hence easy to detect any counterfeits of the coins dated since. Previous to that date the dies were much more irregularly produced, and as a consequence many counterfeits, especially of the Half Dollar, have been made and put in circulation, which the ordinary observer cannot well distingush from those which are good.

The coins of Mexico are particularly obnoxious to this fault. There are seven Mexican mints, each of which uses differently made dies; and in the same mint the dies seem to have often been arbitrarily changed.

Their working dies seem to be made directly from steel punches, for while among many coins many similar items can be identified, their relative position varies somewhat. Perhaps no coin has ever been more extensively and variously counterfeited, during the same length of time, than the Mexican Dollar. This could not have been done, had similarity and regularity prevailed in the dies with which they have been stamped.

The dies used in stamping the coins of the United States at the present time, though very fair, might yet be materially improved, so as to give additional security against a spurious circulation. The very highest order of the die sinking art, should be put in requisition for the production of a series of original dies, which should be adhered to for a long and definite term of years; when, if desirable, they might give place to another series of dies equally elaborate and perfect. The strictest uniformity should also be maintained in respect to the diameter, thickness, and finish of the coins.

V. Counterfeit Coins.

Most counterfeit coins will be found to belong to one of the two following classes: 1st, Those which have been produced by impressions with steel dies. 2nd, Those which have been formed in moulds of plaster, lead, type metal or fusible metal, either by casting, or by the deposition of metal under the influence of galvanism.

1st. *Those that are coined by means of dies.*

Except in a few rare instances where the authentic dies have been stolen, these coins can be detected by comparison with the genuine coin, or a fac simile print thereof, as given in this work. The material commonly used is a debased alloy of silver or gold; silver being combined with an undue proportion of copper, to which is sometimes added zinc, tin, nickel, &c., to improve the color. In cases where the alloy is copper and silver, a good color externally is given to the coin by scrubbing it in aqua ammonia, or boiling it in diluted sulphuric acid, or some other pickling menstruum, which dissolves away the copper and leaves the fine silver. In this way, counterfeits of good appearance are made, which are sonorous, like the genuine coin. They usually range in composition from 150—1000ths to 750—1000ths of fine silver, while genuine Dollar silver has a fineness not far from 900—1000ths. Many of these counterfeits may be detected by cutting or rubbing, as the copper thereby becomes apparent. The energetic action of nitric acid when applied, affords also instructive indications. But the varieties more rich in silver are not thus to be easily distinguished. A careful comparison of stamps is then to be chiefly relied upon. If these false coins are not too bulky, (too large in thickness or diameter,) they are necessarily too light; for silver has a higher specific gravity than copper, and the more coppery an alloy of the two metals is made, the lighter does it become. According to Eckfeldt and Dubois, (Manual of Coins and

Bullion, page 185,) fine or pure silver hammered has a density compared with distilled water as unity of - - - 10.55

Alloyed with copper, and 900—1000ths fine,					10.30
"	"	800	"	"	10.14
"	"	750	"	"	10.05
"	"	700	"	"	9.96
"	"	650	"	"	9.88
"	"	600	"	"	9.80
"	"	550	"	"	9.71
"	"	500	"	"	9.64
Copper,					8.80

Hence, by obtaining the specific gravity of a sonorous silver coin, (directions for doing which may be found in all treatises upon chemistry and natural philosophy,) we may conjecture pretty closely as to the proportion of silver it contains.

The following is a ready and convenient mode of making the density of a Dollar contribute information. Make an upright vessel from the best French plate glass, near three inches high, three inches wide, and rather thicker than the thickest Dollar: the side plates being kept asunder by the interposition of sufficiently thick plate glass, forming the ends. The vessel must then be carefully and minutely graduated as a measure of capacity,after inserting into it a plunger about an inch wide,which is elevated and depressed by a thumb-screw. Have on hand a pair of apothecary's scales and sundry late silver coins of the United States, 900—1000ths fine. Wash the Dollar to be tried in soap suds, and wiping it dry, counterbalance it by the standard silver. Then successively measure the bulk of the standard silver and the Dollar, in the apparatus before described, by observing how far each causes the ascent of water placed therein.

If the Dollar be a ringing counterfeit, containing silver and copper, it will measure more than its own weight of standard silver. The apparatus once in order, a Dollar can be tried in half the time required for reading this account of it.

The method of ascertaining the precise amount of precious metal contained in a coin, is by passing a part of it through the chemical process of assaying, to give a full account of which, would be foreign to the design of this work. It is proper to say, however, that a rude, yet satisfactory assay of silver may thus be made. Wrap, say three grains of the metal to be assayed for silver, in ten or twelve grains of sheet lead, which lay upon a piece of burnt bone, mica, or earthenware, and play upon it the flame of a mouth blow-pipe, until there is nothing left but a globule of pure precious metal. This globule cooled and weighed, will give a fair approximation to the proportion of pure silver present.

2d. *Spurious Coins made in moulds of plaster, lead, type or fusible metal.*

Coins thus made are usually perfect fac-similes of the genuine coins from which they are patterned. The following seems to be one of the villanous plans frequently put in execution. A complete plaster cast is taken from a coin, after the manner in which stereotyping is performed. This is moderately baked and adjusted into a mould into which some alloy of lead, antimony, tin, zinc, &c., analogous to type-metal, is poured in a melted state. When cold, the cast is removed, finished up, and sometimes nicely silvered over. These alloys are too soft, and usually too light, and cannot be made to ring like the genuine coins. Hence they are easy to be detected.

Of late years the curious powers of galvanism have been pressed into the service of counterfeiters. It is probable they first compress the coin into lead, or semifluid fusible metal, to procure accurate types for their business. Upon the types thus formed copper is deposited, under the well known influence of a galvanic current, adapting itself to the most delicate features of the types. When the copper has attained sufficient thickness it is removed from the types, finished up, and the two sides brazed or soldered together, so as to imitate the original coins. Afterwards the whole is delicately silvered over by the same potent means, galvanism. I have seen spurious coins of this sort, that seem to have been deposited in a mould all at one operation, as there were no signs of soldering apparent.

The coins of galvanic production are usually much too light. A person moderately conversant with hard money would instantly perceive the deficiency in weight by merely handling them. It is true the color might be good, and the impression genuine; but a slight cut or scratch would bring to light the copper, and a close inspection, especially with a magnifying glass, would reveal the cheat, by presenting the fine and sharp lines and corners of the impression rounded, blunted, and perhaps partially obliterated, by the deposition thereon of the silver.

MONOGRAPH OF THE DOLLAR.

AMERICAN DOLLARS, OR DOLLARS OF THE UNITED STATES.

The coinage of Dollars in the United States, virtually commencing in 1795, has never been large. The policy of our government has been to issue a great preponderance of halves, and the smaller denominations of coins, under the impression that they would be less likely to be exported from the country.

Up to, and including, the year 1836, the legal weight of the Dollar was 416 grains; its legal fineness, 892$\frac{4}{10}$—1000ths; its value, expressed according to our present standard, is a small fraction less than a dollar, namely, $0.9999854, the deficiency being between one and two hundredths of a mill. By act of Congress, of 18th January, 1837, the present standard of weight and fineness, as before set forth, was established.

No. 1. ***Dollar of the United States.***

Weight, ℥1.010=416.62 grs.=27 grammes, French.
Fineness, 892—1000ths.
Value, $1.001=4*s*. 1.3*d*.=5.34 fr.

No. 2. ***Dollar of the United States.***

Weight, $"1.010=416.62 grs.=27 grms.
Fineness, 893—1000ths. H o r t.
Value, $1.002=4*s.* 1.4*d.*=5.35 fr.

No. 3. ***Dollar of the United States.***

Weight, $"1.010=416.62 grs.=27 grms.
Fineness, 892—1000ths. H o r t.
Value, $1.001=4*s.* 1.3*d.*=5.34 fr.

No. 4. ***Dollar of the United States.***

Weight, $"1.010=416.62 grs.=27 grms.
Fineness, 892—1000ths.
Value, $1.001=4*s.* 1.3*d.*=5.34 fr.

Only 1000 of these dollars were stamped: they are, therefore, rarely met with.

No. 5. ***Dollar of the United States.***

Weight, $"1.000=412.5 grs.=26.72 grms.
Fineness, 900—1000ths.
Value, $1.000=4*s*. 1.3*d*.=5.34 fr.

No counterfeits of the United States Dollar, have come under my observation. Coins seem to be counterfeited just in proportion to the rudeness of their workmanship, and their abundance in general circulation. This dollar has never constituted an important part of the general pecuniary circulation; and the workmanship being comparatively good, it has, I imagine, very seldom been spuriously made.

DOLLAR OF SIERRA LEONE.

Sierra Leone is a colony, founded by a company under English protection, on the western coast of Africa. Neither in weight nor fineness does its nominal dollar bear a reasonably close resemblance to the Spanish dollar; the type of the coins intended to be embraced in this monograph.

No. 6. ***Dollar of Sierra Leone, Africa.***

Weight, $"0.990=408.37 grs.=26.45 grms.
Fineness, 816—1000ths. Bonneville.
Value, $0.900=3*s*. 8.4*d*.=4.81 fr.

SPANISH PENINSULAR DOLLARS.

No. 7. ***Spanish Dollar, of Philip IV., 1691.***
Weight, \$"1.010=416.62 grs.=26.99 grms.
Fineness, 906—1 000ths. B o n n e v i l l e.
Value, \$1,016=4*s*. 2.1*d*.=5.42 fr.

No. 8. ***Spanish Dollar, Charles III.***
Weight, if not worn, \$"1.003=413.73 grs.=26.80 grms.
Fineness, 900—1000ths. E c k f e l d t & D u b o i s.
Value \$1.003=4*s*. 1.5*d*.=5.36 fr.

No. 9. ***Spanish Dollar of Ferdinand VII.***
Weight, \$"1.009. Av. \$"1.004=414 grs.=26.825 grms.
Fineness, 898—1000ths.
Value, \$1,001=4*s*. 1.3*d*.=5.35 fr.

No. 10. ***Spanish Medal Dollar, of Ferd. VII.***
Weight, $"1.000=412.5 grs.=26.72 grms.
Fineness, 900—1000ths.
Value, $1.000=4*s.* 1.3*d.*=5.34 fr.

No. 11. ***Spanish Medal Dollar, Ferd. VII.***
Weight, $"1.004=413 grs.=26.83 grms.
Fineness, probably 900—1000ths.
Value, $1.004=4*s.* 1.5*d.*=5.35 fr. Cabinet of J. M. Kennedy, Esq.

No. 12. ***Spanish Medal Dollar, Ferd. VII.***
Weight. $"1.010=416.6 grs.=26.98 grms.
Fineness, 900—1000ths. ?
Value, $1.010=4*s.* 1.8*d.*=5.39 fr. Cabinet of J. M. Kennedy, Esq.

No. 13. *Spanish Plate Dollar, Ferdinand VII.*
Weight, $"1.009=416.21 grs.=26.96 grms.
Fineness, 898—1000ths. ?
Value, $1.006=4*s.* 1.6*d.*=5.37 fr. Cabinet of the U. S. Mint, at Phil.

No. 14. *Spanish Plate Dollar, Ferdinand VII.*
Weight, $"1.009=416.21 grs.=26.96 grms.
Fineness, 898—1000ths. ?
Value, $1.006=4*s.* 1.6*d.*=5.37 fr. Cabinet of the U. S. Mint, Phil.

No. 15. *Spanish Dollar, Barcelona.*
Weight, $"1.001. Av. $"0.980.=404 grs.=26.175 grms.
Fineness, 896—1000ths.
Value, av. $0.975=4*s.*=5.21 fr.

No. 16. *Spanish Dollar of Ferdinand VII.*
Weight, $"1.004=414 grs.=26.825 grms.
Fineness, 898—1000ths.
Value, $1.001=4*s.* 1.3*d.*=5.35 fr.

No. 17. *Spanish Dollar of Joseph Napoleon,* 1812.
Weight, $"1.012, av. $"1.006=415 grs.=26.89 grms.
Fineness, 900—1000ths. Eckf. & Dubois.
Value, $1.006=4*s.* 1.6*d.*=5.37 fr.

No. 18. *Spanish Dollar of Ferdinand.*
Weight, $"1.000, av. $"1.003=414 grs.=26.825 grms.
Fineness, 900—1000ths.
Value, $1.003=4*s.* 1.5*d.*=5.36 fr.

No. 19. ***Spanish Dollar, of Isabella II.***
Weight, $\$^{w}$1.010=416.62 grs.=26.99 grms.
Fineness, 900—1000ths.
Value, $\$$1.010=4*s.* 1.8*d*=5.39 fr.

SPANISH AMERICAN DOLLARS.

These Dollars, embodying most of the vast amounts of silver formerly produced from the mines of Mexico and South America, are known in every region of the earth, where money is valued. Hence, the Spanish Dollar may be regarded almost as a universal unit, or integer of money. It is fortunate that our Dollar of the United States, approaches it in quality, weight and value so nearly.

In the present day, the Mexican and South American Dollars, are for obvious reasons, taking its place.

No. 20. ***Spanish American Cob Dollar.***
Weight, $\$^{w}$1,010=416.62 grs.=26.99 grms.
Fineness, 903—1000ths.
Value, $\$$.1013=4*s.* 1.9*d.*=5.47 fr.

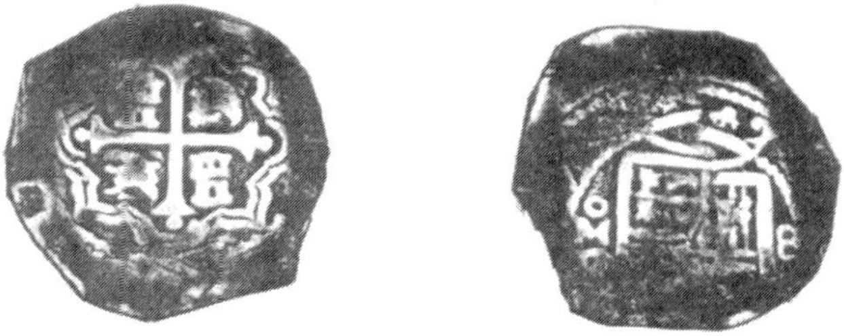

No. 21. ***Spanish American Cob Dollar.***

Weight, $"0.990=408.37 grs.=26.45 grms.
Fineness, 903—1000ths.
Value, $0.993=4*s.* 0.9*d.*=5.30 fr.

No. 22. ***Spanish Amer. Globe Dollar of Charles III.***

Mint of Mexico.

Weight, $"1.015, av. $"0.996=411 grs.=26.628 grms.
Fineness, 910—1000ths. Value, av. $1.008=4*s.* 1.8*d.*=5.38 fr.

No. 23. ***Spanish Amer. Pillar Dollar, Charles III.***

Mint of Mexico.

Weight, $"1.012, av. $"1.010=416.62 grs.=27 grms.
Fineness, 898—1000ths. Eckfeldt & Dubois.
Value, $1.007=4*s.* 1.7*d.*=5.38 fr.

These coins are generally worn, and hence weigh less than above stated.

No. 24. ***Spanish American Dollar of Charles IV.***

Mint of Mexico. Impressed with Chinese characters.

Weight, \$"0999½, av. wt. \$"1.001=413 grs.=26.75 grms.
Fineness, 898—1000ths.
Value, \$0.998=4*s*. 0.7*d*.=5.29 fr.

No. 25. ***Spanish American Dollar of Charles IV.***

Mint of Mexico.

Weight, \$"0.999, av. \$"1.001.=413 grs.=26.75 grms.
Fineness, 898—1000ths.
Value, \$0.998=4*s*. 0.7*d*.=5.29 f..

No. 26. ***Spanish American Dollar, Ferd. VII.***

Mint of Mexico.

Weight, \$"1.010.=416.62 grs.=26.99 grms.
Fineness, 898—1000ths. Eckfeldt & Dubois.
Value, \$1.007=4*s*. 1.7*d*.=5.38fr.

The worn coins of this stamp weigh less than above stated.

No. 27. *Spanish American Dollar, Ferd. VII.*
Mint of Lima, Peru.

Weight, $"1.010=416.62 grs.=26.99 grms.
Fineness, 898—1000ths. E c k f e l d t & D u b o i s.
Value, $1.007=4*s.* 1.7*d.*=5.38 fr.

No. 28. *Spanish American Dollar, Ferd. VII.*
Mint of Lima, Peru.

Weight, $"1.010=416.62 grs.=26.99 grms.
Fineness, 900—1000ths.
Value. $1.010=4*s.* 1.8*d*=5.39 fr.

No. 29. *Spanish Dollar, restamped in England.*

Weight, $"1.000—412.50 grs.=26.72 grms.
Fineness, 900—1000ths.
Value, $1.000=4*s.* 1.3*d.*=5.34 fr.

VARGAS, MORELOS, HAMMERED AND HISPA-NO-MEXICAN DOLLARS.

The coins which follow, were manufactured within the territory of Mexico, from the year 1810 to 1822, during the period of the Revolutionary War with Spain, which resulted in the Independence of Mexico. Most of them are very rudely made, and most of them bear the royal effigy, arms, or Legend of Ferd. VII., though necessarily made without his authority.

Those Dollars which I have designated Hispano-Mexican, the Hammered, and also the Vargas Dollars, are still very abundant in this part of the world, (New Orleans,) being usually admixed to the extent of 4 or 5 per cent. in all large lots of Mexican Dollars. About $50,000 of them per annum, arrive at the New Orleans mint for re-coinage.

No. 30. ***Rude and Unique Mexican Dollar.***

Weight $°0.840=346.50 grs.=22.45 grms.
Fineness, near 900—1000ths. (?)
Value $0.840=3*s.* 5.4*d.*=4.49 fr

EXPL.—*Obverse.* An arch of masonry sustaining the prickly pear, upon which stands a crowned eagle or owl. Legend, Ferdinand dei gratia 1811. Inscription, 8. R. *Reverse.* A hand holding a bow and arrow, a quiver, spear and hunting bag. Legend, Provisional por la Suprema junta de America. Edged after the style of Spanish Dollars.

No. 31. ***Mexican Morelos Dollar*, 1813.**

Weight, $°0.990=408.37 grs.=26.45 grms.
Fineness, 880—1000ths. Eckfeldt & Dubois.
Value, $0.968=3*s.* 11.7*d.*=5.17 fr. Cabinet of Philadelphia U. S. Mint.

No. 32. *Mexican Hammered Dollar, Gen. Vargas, Sombrerete,* 1812.

Weight, $0.980=404.25 grs.=26.19 grms.
Fineness, 883—1000ths, average. Hort.
Value, $0.963=3*s.* 11.4*d.*=5.14 fr.

No. 33. *Mexican Hammered Dollar, Zacatecas,* 1811, (a.)

Weight, $0.980=404.25 grs.=26.19 grms.
Fineness, 875—1000ths, average.
Value, $0.952=3*s.* 10.9*d.*=5.09 fr.
These dollars vary from 530 to 996—1000ths, in fineness. Hort.

No. 34. *Mexican Hammered Dollar, Zacatecas,* 1811, (b.)

Weight, $1.020=420.75 grs.=27.26 grms.
Fineness, 875—1000ths. Value, $0.991=4*s.* 0.8*d.*=5.29 fr.

No. 35. ***Mexican Sand Dollar, moulded in sand from a Spanish Dollar*, 1811.**

Weight, $"0.990=408.37 grs.=26.45 grms.
Fineness, 916—1000ths. Hort. Value, $1.007=4*s*. 1.6*d*.=5.37 fr.

This assay was made by Dr. Hort from ten Sand Dollars melted together.

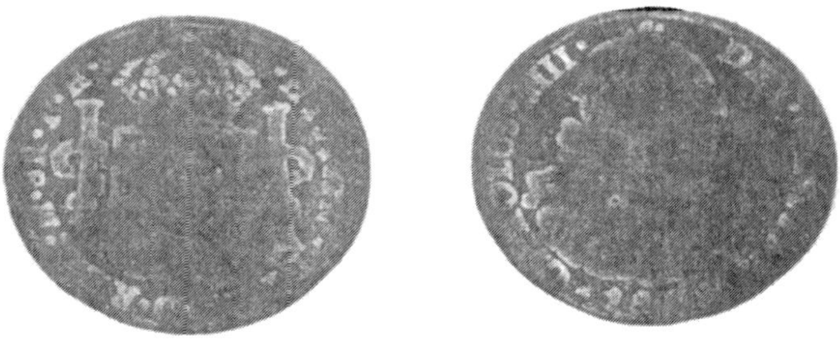

No. 36. ***Mexican Sand Dollar, moulded from a Spanish Dollar. Charles IV.*, 1808.**

Weight, $"0.830.
Fineness, near 916—1000ths. Value, $0.844.

Rare. The Sand Dollars usually bear Ferdinand VII. 1811 or 1812, in the legend.

No. 37. ***Mexican Hammered Dollar.***

Weight, $"0.980=404 grs.=26.19 grms.
Fineness, 880—1000ths. Value, $0.958=3*s*. 11.2*d*.=5 12 fr.

No. 38. ***Mexican Hammered Dollar.***

Weight, $"0.970=400.12 grs.=25.92 grms.
Fineness, 880—1000ths.
Value, $0.948=3*s.* 10.7*d.*=5.06 fr.

No. 39. ***Mexican Hammered Dollar.***

Weight, $"0.970.=400 grs.=25.92 grms.
Fineness, 880—1000ths.
Value, $0.948=3*s.* 10.7*d.*=5.06 fr.

No. 40. ***Mexican Hammered Dollar.***

Weight, $"0.980=404.25 grs.=26.19 grms.
Fineness, 880—1000ths.
Value, $0.958=3*s.* 11.2*d.*=5.12 fr.

No. 41. ***Mexican Hammered Dollar, made in the time of the Mexican Revolution.***

Weight, $"1.010=416.6 grs.=26.98 grms.
Fineness, 880—1000ths.
Value, $0.987=4*s.* 0.7*d.*=5.28 fr.

No. 42. ***Mexican Hammered Dollar***

Mint of Zacatecas.

Weight, $"1.000=412.50 grs.=26.72 grms.
Fineness, 890—1000ths.
Value, $0.990=4*s.* 0.8*d.*=5.29 fr.

No. 43. ***Hispano-Mexican Dollar.***

Weight, $"0.980=404=25 grs.=26.19 grms.
Fineness, 898—1000ths.
Value, $0.977=4*s.*=5.21 fr.

No. 44. ***Hispano-Mexican Dollar.***

Mint of Zacatecas.

Weight, $"1.000=412.50 grs.=26.72 grms.
Fineness, 900.—1000ths.
Value, $1.000=4*s*. 1.3*d*.=5.34 fr.

COUNTERFEIT SPANISH AMERICAN DOLLARS, CHARLES III.

No. 45. ***Spanish American Ct. Dollar, Charles III. Mexico,* 1778**

Weight, $"0.900.
Fineness, near **230**—1000ths.
Value, $0.230.

No. 46. ***Spanish American Ct. Charles III. Mexico*, 1781.**

Weight, $"0.900.
Fineness, near 360—1000ths. Value, $0.360.

No. 47. ***Spanish American, Low Standard, Charles III. Mexico*, 1783.**

Weight, $"0.870.
Fineness, near 450—1000ths. Value, $0.435.

No. 48. ***Spanish American Ct., Charles III.***

Mint of Mexico.

Weight, $"0.900. Fineness, 5—1000ths. Hort. Value, $0.005.
Copper silvered over.

COUNTERFEIT SPANISH AMERICAN DOLLARS, CHARLES IV.

In reference to Nos. 59 to 64, inclusive, bearing date from 1811 to 1824, it may be remarked, that no genuine Dollar of Charles (Carolus, Latin,) IV. is dated later than 1808.

No. 49. ***Spanish American Ct., Charles IV. Mexico,*** **1787.**

Weight, 8"0.990.
Fineness, near 380—1000ths.
Value, $0.418.

No. 50. ***Spanish American Ct., Charles IV., Mexico,*** **1789.**

Weight, 8"1.000.
Fineness, 15—1000ths.
Value, $0.016.

Copper, silvered over.

No. 51. *Span. American Dollar, Low Standard Charles IV. Mexico,* 1800.

Weight, $1"1.010.
Fineness, 354—1000ths. Hort.
Value, $0.397.

No. 52. *Spanish American Ct., Charles IV. Mexico,* 1801. (a.)

Weight, $"0.950.
Fineness, 317—1000ths. Hort.
Value, $0.334.

No. 53. *Spanish American Ct., Charles IV.* 1801. (b.)

Weight, $"0.960.
Fineness, 225—1000ths. Hort.
Value, $0.240.

No. 54. ***Spanish American Ct., Charles IV. Mexico*, 1802.**

Weight, $"1.030.
Fineness, near 264—1000ths. Value, $0.302.

No. 55. ***Spanish American Ct., Charles IV. Mexico*, 1805,** (a.)

Weight, $"0.940.
Fineness, near 270—1000ths. Value, $0.282.

No. 56. ***Span. American Dollar, Low Standard, Charles IV. Mexico*, 1805.** (b.)

Weight, $"0.950. m
Fineness, near 500—1000ths. Value, $0.527.

No. 57. ***Span. American Dollar, Low Standard, Charles IV. 1808.*** (a.)

Weight, $"0.990.
Fineness, near 450—1000ths.
Value, $0.485.

No. 58. ***Spanish American Dollar, Low Standard, Charles IV. Mexico, 1808.*** (b.)

Weight, $"1.000
Fineness, near 500—1000ths.
Value, $0.555.

No. 59. ***Spanish American Ct., Charles IV. Mexico, 1811.***

Weight, $"0.860.
Fineness, near 670—1000ths. Value $0.640.

No. 60. ***Spanish American Ct., Charles IV. Mexico*, 1813.**

Weight, $"0.950.
Fineness, near 330—1000ths.
Value, $0.348.

No. 61. ***Spanish American Ct., Charles IV. Mexico*, 1818.** (a.)

Weight, $"0.870.
Fineness, 200—1000ths. Hort. Value, $0.193.

No. 62. ***Spanish American Ct., Charles IV. Mexico*, 1818.** (b.)

Weight, $."0.980.
Fineness, near 450—1000ths. Value, $0.490.

No. 63. ***Spanish American Ct., Charles IV. Mexico,* 1822.**

Weight, ℥1.060.
Fineness, near 280—1000ths.
Value, $0.329.

No. 64. ***Spanish American Dollar, Ct., Charles IV. Mexico,* 1824.**

Weight, ℥0.960.
Fineness, 312—1000ths. Hort.
Value, $0.332.

LOW STANDARD AND COUNTERFEIT HAMMERED DOLLARS, AND LOW STANDARD AND COUNTERFEIT HISPANO-MEXICAN DOLLARS, OF FERDINAND VII.

Nos. 65 to 79, inclusive.

Many of these coins were doubtless made by the same hands that produced the better sorts of hammered Dollars. They were carelessly, and, perhaps, fraudulently made, containing much more silver in some instances than ordinary counterfeits.

Some of them, it is obvious, are base and intentional counterfeits.

No. 65. ***Mexican Hammered Dollar, Low Standard. Zacatecas,*** **1811.** (c.)
Weight, $"0.820.
Fineness, 530—1000ths. Hort. Value, **$0.482.** [Vide, No. 33.]

No. 66. ***Mexican Hammered Dollar, Low Standard. Zacatecas,*** **1811.** (d.)
Weight, $"0.950. Fineness, near **540—1000ths.**
Value, $0.570. [Vide No. 33.]

No. 67. ***Hammered Dollar, Counterfeit.***
Weight, $"0.960. Fineness, 175—1000ths Value, **$0.186.**

No. 68. ***Hammered Dollar, Low Stand., Mexico.***
Weight, $"0.010.
Fineness, near 490—1000ths. Value, $0.550.

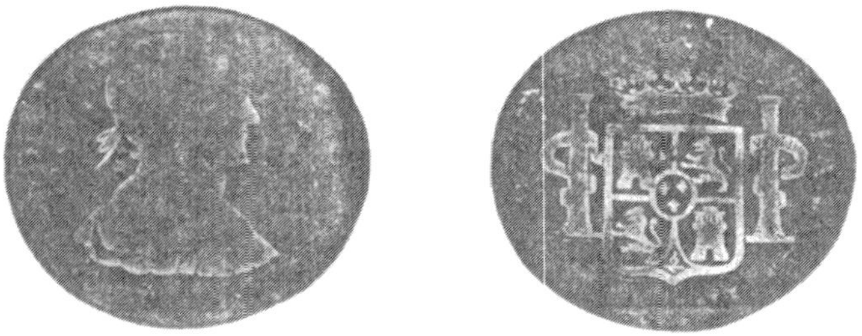

No. 69. ***Hammered Dollar, Low Stand., Mexico.***
Weight, $"0.970.
Fineness, near 450—1000ths. Value, $0.485.

No. 70. ***Hispano-Mexican Ct., Mexico.***
Weight, $"0.880.
Fineness, near 390—1000ths. Value, $0.381.

No. 71. ***Hispano-Mexican, Low Stand., Mexico.***

Weight, $"0.980. Fineness, near 690—1000ths. Value, $0.751.

No. 72. ***Hispano-Mexican, Counterfeit, Mexico.***

Appears as if cast.

Weight, $"0.890. Fineness, near 200—1000ths. Value, $0.197.

No. 73. ***Hispano-Mexican, Low Standard, Zacatecas.***

Weight, $"0.890. Fineness, near 700—1000ths. Value, $0.692.

No. 74. ***Hispano-Mexican Counterfeit.***
Weight, $"1.000.
Fineness, near 560—1000ths.
Value, $0.622.

No. 75. ***Hispano-Mexican Ct. Zacatecas.***
Weight, $"0.950. Fineness, near 600—1000ths. Value, $0.633.

No. 76. ***Hispano-Mexican Ct. Mexico.***
Weight, $"0.940. Fineness, near 250—1000ths. Value, $0.261.

No. 77. ***Hispano-Mexican Ct. Dollar, Zacatecas,* 1821.**

Weight, $^{-}0.930. Fineness, 312—1000ths. Hort. Value, $0.322.

No. 78. ***Hisp.-Mexican Dollar, Low Standard, Guanaxuato,* 1822.**

Weight, $^{-}0.940. Fineness, 677—1000ths. Hort. Value, $0.707.

No. 79. ***Hispano-Mexican Ct., Zacatecas.***

Weight, $^{-}0.990. Fineness, near 285—1000ths. Value, $0.313.

BRAZILIAN DOLLARS.

Nos. 80 to 89.

The Brazilian Dollars, previous to 1833, were evidently made by re-stamping current Spanish American Dollars, with the national arms and devices of Portugal and Brazil. The Spanish crown, pillars, legend, &c., may generally be faintly seen, not having been completely erased by the process of annealing and stamping.

This cheap mode of getting up a national coinage, had its evils, since it is apparent that counterfeit Spanish Dollars have thus often been restamped.

No. 80. ***Spanish Dollar re-stamped in Brazil.***

Weight, $"1.005=414 grs.=26.82 grms.
Fineness, 900—1000ths.
Value, $1.005=4*s.* 1.6*d.*=5.36 fr.

No. 81. ***Spanish Dollar re-stamped in Brazil.***

Weight, $"1.007=415.38 grs.=26.90 grms.
Fineness, 900—1000ths,
Value, $1.007=4*s.* 1.7*d.*=5.38 fr.

No. 82. ***Spanish Dollar, Ct., impressed with the genuine Brazilian stamp.***

Weight, \$·0.945=389.75 grs.=25.25 grms.
Fineness, near 200—1000ths. Value, \$0.210=0*s.* 10.3*d.*=1.12 fr.

No. 83. ***Spanish Dollar, marked by Brazilian Stamps.***

Weight, \$·1.001=413 grs.=26.75 grms.
Fineness, 898—1000ths. Value, \$0.998=4*s.* 0.7*d.*=5.29 fr.

No. 84. ***Spanish Dollar, re-stamped in Brazil.***

Considerably worn.

Weight, \$·0.940=387.75 grs.=25.12 grms.
Fineness, 900—1000ths. Value, \$0.940=3*s.* 10.3*d.*=5.02 fr.

No. 85. ***Spanish Dollar restamped in Brazil.***
Weight, $"1.007=415,38 grs.=26.90 grms.
Fineness, 900—1000ths.
Value, $1.007=4*s*.1.7*d*.=5.38 fr.

No. 86. ***Counterfeit Spanish Dollar, impressed with the Genuine Brazilian stamp.***
Weight, $"0.93. Fineness, near 630—1000ths. Value, $0.651.

No. 87. ***Piece of* 960 *Reis. Brazil. Spanish Dollar restamped.***
Weight, $"1.000=412.50 grs=26.72 grms.
Fineness, 900—1000ths.
Value, $1.000=4*s*. 1.3*d*.=5.34 fr

No. 88. ***Brazil. Spanish Dollar restamped. Piece of 960 Reis***

Weight, $"1.000.=412.50 grs.=26.72 grms.
Fineness, 900—1000ths.
Value, $1.000=4*s.* 1.3*d.*=5.34 fr.

No. 89. ***Brazilian Dollar.* 1200 *Reis.***

Weight, $"1.000.=412.50 grs.=26.72 grms.
Fineness, 891—1000ths. E c k f e l d t & D u b o i s.
Value, $0.990=4*s.* 0.8*d.*=5.29 fr.

DOLLARS OF THE SOUTH AMERICAN REPUBLICS.

While the region now embraced in the various South American Republics was dependent on Spain, the silver, produced and coined, bore the impress of the pillars and royal bust, of the coinage of Spanish America. The republican money which succeeded, was intended to maintain the same standards of weight and fineness. But, really, in these respects, some very great irregularities have been found to prevail.

6

No. 90. ***Peruvian Dollar.***

Mint of Lima.

Weight, $"1.010=416.62 grs.=27 grms.
Fineness, 901—1000ths. Eckfeldt & Dubois.
Value, $1.011=4*s*. 1.8*d*.=5.39fr.

No. 91. ***Peruvian Dollar. Restampted by the Royalists.***

Mint of Lima.

Weight, value, and fineness, like No. 90.

No. 92. ***Peruvian Dollar.***

Mint of Cuzco.

Weight, $"1.010=416.62 grs.=27 grms.
Fineness, 901—1000ths.
Value, $1,011=4*s*. 1.8*d*.=5.39 fr.

No. 93. ***Peruvian Dollar.***

Mint of Lima.

Weight, 8'' 0.990=408.37 grs.=**26.45** grms.
Fineness, 901—1000ths. Value, **$0.991**.=**4**s. **0.8**d.=**5.29** fr.

No. 94. ***Debased Peruvian Dollar.***

Mint of Lima.

Weight, 8'' 0.980=404.25 grs.=**26.19** grms.
Fineness, near **510—1000**ths. Value, **$0.555=2**s. **3.4**d.=**2.97** fr.

No. 95. ***Peruvian Dollar.***

Mint of Lima.

Weight, 80''.990=408.37 grs.=**26.45** grms.
Fineness, 901—1000ths.
Value, $0.991=4s. **0.8**d.=**5.29** fr.

No. 96. ***Peruvian Dollar.***

Mint of Cuzco.

Weight, $"1.010=416.62 grs.=27 grms.
Fineness, 901—1000ths. Value, $1.011=4*s*. 1.8*d*.=5.39 fr.

No. 97. ***Peruvian Dollar.***

Weight, $"1.012=417.62 grs.=27.05 grms.
Fineness, 900—1000ths. Value $1.012=4*s*. 1.9*d*=5.41 fr.

No. 98. ***Debased Peruvian Dollar.***

Mint of Lima.

Weight, $"0.970=400.12 grs.=25.92 grms.
Fineness, 510—1000ths. Hort. Value, $0.550=2*s*. 3.1*d*.=2.94 fr.
A similar Dollar observed of date 1829.

No. 99. ***Peruvian Dollar.***

Mint of Cuzco, 1837.

Weight, 8ᵛ1.003=413.73 grs.=**26.80** grms.
Fineness, 904—1000ths.
Value, $1.007=4s. 1.6*d.*=**5.37** fr.

No. 100. ***Debased Peruvian Dollar.***

Mint of Cuzco.

Weight, 8ᵛ0.830=342.37 grs.=**22.18** grs.
Fineness, 510—1000ths. H o r t .
Value, $0.470=1s. **11.1***d.*=**2.51** fr.

No. 101. ***Peruvian Dollar.***

Mint of Cuzco, 1838.

Weight, 8ᵛ1.003=414grs.=**26.82** grms.
Fineness, 904—1000ths. E c k f e l d t & D u b o i s .
Value, $1.007=4s. **1.6***d.*=**5.37** fr.

No. 102. ***North Peruvian Dollar.***
Weight, $"1.012=417.62 grs.=27.05 grms.
Fineness, 900—1000ths. Hort. Value, $1.012.=4*s.* 1.9*d.*=5.41 fr.

No. 103. ***Debased Peruvian Dollar. North Peru,* 1838.**
With the Central American small stamp affixed. Mint of Lima.
Weight, $"1.010=416.62 grs.=27 grms.
Fineness, near 540—1000ths. Value, $0.606=2*s.* 5.9*d.*=3.24 fr.

No. 104. ***Peruvian Dollar.* 1840.**
Mint of Cuzco.
Weight, $"1.004=414.15 grs.=26.82 grms.
Fineness, 899—1000ths. Value, $1.002=4*s.* 1.4*d.*=5.35 fr.

No. 105. ***Peruvian Dollar.* 1841.**

Mint of Lima.

Weight, $"1.010=416.62. grs.=**27** grms.
Fineness, 899—1000ths. Eckfeldt & Dubois.
Value, $1.008.=4*s*. 1.6*d*. 5.37 fr.

No. 106. ***Peruvian Dollar.***

Mint of Lima.

Weight, $"1.011=417 grs.=27.019 grms.
Fineness, 900—1000ths. Hort. Value, **$1.011=4*s*. 1.8*d*.=5.39 fr.**

No. 107. ***Chilian Dollar*, 1817.**
Weight, $"0.990.=408.37 grs.=26.45 grms.
Fineness, 907—1000ths. Eckfeldt & Dubois.
Value, $0.997=4*s*. 1.1*d*.=5.33 fr.

No. 108. *Chilian Dollar.* 1833.

Weight, $"1.00=414 grs.=26.82 grms,
Fineness, 907—1000ths. E c k f e l d t & D u b o i s.
Value, $1.011=4*s.* 1.8*d.*=5.39 fr.

No. 109. *Chilian Dollar.*

Weight, $"1.004=414 grs.=26.82 grms.
Fineness, 907—1000ths. E c k f e l d t & D u b o i s.
Value, $1.011=4*s.* 1.8*d.*=5.39 fr.

No. 110. *Dollar of Rio de LaPlata.*

Weight, $"1.000=412.50 grs =26.72 grms.
Fineness, average, 820—1000ths (?)
Value $0.911=3*s.* 8.9*d.*=4.86 fr.

No. 111. ***Dollar of the Argentine Republic, South America.***

Weight, $"0.970.=400 grs.=**26** grms.
Fineness, 928—1000ths, Eckfeldt & Dubois.
Value, $1.000=4s. 1.3d.=**5.34** fr.

No. 112. ***Colombian Dollar.***

Weight, $"0.850.=350.6 grs.=**22.71** grms.
Fineness, 730—1000ths. Eck. & Dubois. **736—1000ths.** Hort.
Value, $0.695.=2s. 10.2d.=**3.72** fr., by Hort's assay.

No. 113. ***Colombian Dollar.***

Weight, $"1.011=417 grs.=**26.99** grms.
Fineness, 910—1000ths. Eckfeldt & Dubois.
Value, $1.022=4s. 2.4d.=5.46 fr.

No. 114. ***Colombian Dollar.***
Weight, $"0.900=371 grs.=24 grms.
Fineness, 680—1000ths. Eckfeldt & Dubois.
Value, $0.680=2*s.* 9.5*d.*=5.63 fr.

BOLIVIAN DOLLARS.

No. 115. ***Bolivian Dollar.***
Weight, $"1.010=416.62 grs.=27 grms.
Fineness, 902—1000ths. Eckfeldt & Dubois.
Value, $1.012=4*s.* 1.8*d.*=5.40 fr.

No. 116. ***Debased Bolivian Dollar.***
Stamp apparently genuine.
Weight, $"1.030=424.87 grs.=27.52 grms.
Fineness, 682—1000ths. Hort. Value, $0.780=3*s.* 2.5*d.*=4.17 fr.

No. 117. ***Debased Bolivian Dollar.***

Stamp apparently genuine.

Weight, oz. 0.980=404 grs.=26.19 grms.
Fineness, 682—1000ths. Hort. Value, $0.742=3*s.* 0.6*d.*=3.97 fr.

Dollars of similar stamp and quality have been observed, bearing date, 1834, 1837, 1838.

No. 118. ***Bolivian Dollar.***

Weight, oz. 1.003=413.73 grs.=26.80 grms.
Fineness, 907—1000ths. Hort. Value, $1.010=4*s.* 1.8*d.*=5.40 fr.

DOLLAR OF CENTRAL AMERICA.

No. 119. ***Central American Dollar.***

Mint of New Guatemala.

Weight, oz. 1.003=415 grs.=26.89 grms.
Fineness, 896—1000ths. Eckfeldt & Dubois.
Value, $1.001=4*s.* 1.3*d.*=5.34 fr.

No. 120. ***Central American Dollar, Ct.***

Weight, $"1.010. Fineness, near 5—1000ths. Value, $0.005.

Type made from a broken coin. Copper washed with silver. Coin remarkably thick.

MEXICAN DOLLARS.

More than 90 per cent. of the Dollars in general circulation in this country, bear the Mexican stamp. This arises from two facts: 1st. There is far more silver produced from the mines of Mexico, than from the mines of all the world besides: 2d. It is, and has been, the policy of that government, to prevent the export of uncoined bullion, the government deriving a large revenue from its coinage, amounting, I have been informed, to 10 per cent. During the days of Spanish rule, near $23,000,000 in silver were annually obtained from the mines; since the Mexican independence probably $15,000,000 would more nearly express the annual amount. The Mexican Dollar, at the present day, holds the place in the commerce of the world, held forty years ago by the famous Spanish American Pillar Dollar.

The style of workmanship in which they are executed is not of the best, and no regular system seems to have been pursued, with a view to render the detection of counterfeits easy.

I have expended an amount of labor, and exercised a degree of patience, commensurate I think with the importance of the matter, in seeking out, and comparing every accessible variety of impressions, borne by the genuine Mexican Dollar; by a contrast with which, counterfeits may generally be at once detected. The fac-simile impressions of the same, which follow, are classified by the mint marks, in the legend, immediately at the left hand of the dates—preceding the same. Thus,

Ṁ.—Mint of the City of Mexico.
E^{o} M^{o}—Apparently the same.
GC—Apparently the same.
Z^{s}—Mint of Zacatecas.
G^{o}—Mint of Guanaxuato.
D^{o}—Mint of Durango.
P^{i}—Mint of San Luis Potosi.
C^{A}—Mint of Chihuahua.
G^{A}—Mint of Guadalaxara.
H^{o}—Mint unknown to me.

The letters, usually two, which are on the right hand of the date, following it, are probably the initials of the moneyer or master of the mint.

In comparing coins with the following fac-similes, for the purpose of detecting counterfeits, the relative importance of the different parts of the impression ought to be always borne in mind. From comparing many Mexican coins, it seems pretty certain to me that the eagle, snake, cactus, earth and water of the one side, and the liberty cap and rays of the other, have generally been impressed into the dies from permanent king dies ; and the letters and figures of the legends have afterwards been separately impressed. In most instances the wreaths which arise from the water and ascend in the legend, each side of the cactus, seem also to have belonged to the king die. The spines of the cactus seem to have been separately superadded. Now in performing a large coinage the dies used in stamping the silver or gold seldom endure more than ten days active service, when they have to be replaced by new ones made as before described, from the king dies, etc. Hence there is not always that perfect coincidence, in the relative position of the letters, figures, spines, and other parts, which is desirable. Nevertheless, having prepared types of every essential variety that has fallen under my notice, I trust they will be found adequate to the object intended, the ready and easy detection of spurious coins. For when a die of any complication is cut in steel *de novo*, it is probably beyond the power of human art so well to imitate another die as to produce a perfect fac-simile. If the unassisted eye can descry no difference, dissimilarities will be made apparent by nice measurements and the magnifying glass.

GENUINE MEXICAN DOLLARS OF THE MINT OF MEXICO.

Mint Mark, M̊. **or** E°. M°. **or** GC.

No. 121. ***Iturbide Dollar.***

Mint of Mexico. This stamp bears date 1822 or 1823.

Weight, •1.010=416.26 grs.=26.993 grms.
Fineness, 898—1000ths. Eckfeldt & Dubois.
Value, $1.007=4s. 1.6*d.*=5.37 fr.

No. 122. ***Iturbide Dollar.***

Mint of Mexieo.

This stamp bears date 1822 or 1823.

Weight, $"1.010=416.26 grs.=26.993 grms.
Fineness, 898—1000ths. Eckfeldt & Dubois.
Value, $1.007=4*s.* 1.6*d.*=5.37 fr.

Ten of these coins taken indiscriminately weighed 269.40 grms.

For counterfeits see Nos. 183, 184, 185, 186.

No. 123. ***Mexican Medal Dollar of Iturbide.***

Weight $"1.030=424.87 grs.=27.52 grms.
Fineness, near 900—1000ths.
Value, $1.030=4*s.* 2.8*d.*=5.50 fr.

No. 124. ***Hook-Neck Dollar.***

Mint of Mexico.

Weight, $"1.010=416.26 grs.=26.993 grms.
Fineness, 898—1000ths.
Value, $1.007=4*s.* 1.6*d.*=5.37 fr.

No. 125. ***Hook-Neck Dollar.***

Mint of Mexico.

Weight, $"1.010=416.26 grs.=**26.993** fr.
Fineness, 898—1000ths.
Value, $1.007=4*s*. 1.6*d*.=**5.37** fr.

For Counterfeits, see Nos. 188, 191, 192, 193.

No. 126. ***Hook-Neck Dollar.***

Mint of Mexico.

Weight, $"1.010=416.26 grs.=**26.993** grms.
Fineness, 898—1000ths.
Value, $1.007=4*s*. 1.6*d*.=**5.37** fr.

For Counterfeits, see Nos. 188, 191, 192, 193.

No. 127. ***Dollar.***

Mint of Mexico.

Weight, $"1.007=415.38 grs.=**26.90** grms.
Fineness, 898—1000ths.
Value, $1.004=4*s*. 1.5*d*.=**5.36** fr.

For Counterfeits, see Nos. 187, 189, 190.

No. 128. ***Dollar.***

Mint of Mexico.

Weight, $"1.010=416.26 grs.=26.993 grms.
Fineness, 900—1000ths.
Value, $1.010=4*s.* 1.8*d*=5.39 fr.

This stamp, with little essential change, runs through a series of twenty years, to the present time, 1845. For Counterfeits, see Nos. 194 to 205, inclusive.

No. 129. ***Dollar.***

Mint of Mexico.

Weight, $"1.011=417 grs.=27.019 grms.
Fineness, 900—1000ths. Hort.
Value, $1.011=4*s.* 1.8*d.*=5.39 fr.

This stamp runs from 1826 to 1842. The Dollars of 1825, 1843, 1844, 1845, differ but little from it. For Counterfeits, see Nos. 197 to 211, inclusive.

No. 130. ***Dollar.*** Mint of Mexico.

Weight, $"1.011=417 grs.=27.019 grms.
Fineness, 900—1000ths. Hort. Value, $1.011=4*s.* 1.8*d.*=5.39 fr.

No. 131. ***Dollar.*** Mint of Mexico.

Stamp of 1845. For Weight, Fineness and Value, see stamp of 1842, No. 129.

No. 132. ***Mexican Dollar. Mint Mark,*** EoMo

The stamp appears identical with that of the Mint of Mexico.

Weight, $"1.011=417 grs.=**27.019** grms.
Fineness, 897—1000ths. Hort.
Value, $1.0007=4*s.* 1.6*d.*=**5.37** fr.

For Counterfeit, see No. 405.

No. 133. ***Mexican Dollar. Mint Mark,*** GC.

Stamp that of the Mint of Mexico.

Weight, $"1.005.
Fineness, 904—1000ths. Hort.
Value, $1.009. 8

GENUINE MEXICAN DOLLARS.

Mint of Zacatecas. Mint Mark, Z^s

No. 134. ***Mexican Dollar.***

Mint of Zacatecas. Stamp of 1825.

Weight, $"0.990=408.37 grs.=26.45 grms.
Fineness, 890—1000ths. Hort.
Value, $0.979=4*s.* 0.1*d.*=5.23 fr. For Counterfeit, see No. 213.

No. 135. ***Mexican Dollar.***

Mint of Zacatecas. Stamp of 1826, in part.

Weight, $"1.000=412.5 grs.=26.72 grms.
Fineness, 895—1000ths.
Value, $0.994=4*s.* 1*d.*=5.31 fr. For Counterfeit, See No. 214.

No. 136. ***Mexican Dollar.***

Mint of Zacatecas. Stamp of 1826, (in part,) to 1835, inclusive.

Weight, $"1.004=414.15 grs.=26.83 grms.
Fineness, 895—1000ths. Value, $0.998=4*s.* 1.2*d.*=5.33 fr.

Weight and title varying considerably, but the above is a fair average. For Counterfeits, see No. 214 to 246, inclusive.

No. 137. ***Mexican Dollar.***

Mint of Zacatecas. Stamp of 1836 to 1841, inclusive.

Weight, $"1.010=416.26 grs.=**26.993** grms.
Fineness, 896—1000ths., average. Value, **$1.005=4***s.* 1.5*d.*=5.37 fr.

For Counterfeits, see Nos. 247 to 270, inclusive.

No. 138. ***Mexican Dollar.***

Mint of Zacatecas. Stamp of 1842, 1843, 1844, 1845.

Weight, $"1.004=414.15 grs.=26.83 grms.
Fineness, 898—1000ths. Hort.
Value, $1.002=4*s.* 1.4*d.*=5.35 fr. For Cts., see Nos. 272 to 281, inclusive.

GENUINE MEXICAN DOLLARS.
Mint of Guanaxuato. Mint Mark, G°

No. 139. ***Hook-Neck Dollar.***

Mint of Guanaxuato. Stamp of 1824, 1825.

Weight, $"1.010=416.26 grs=26.993 grms.
Fineness, 899—1000ths. Value, **$1.008=4***s.* 1.7*d.*=5.38 fr.

No. 140. ***Mexican Dollar.***

Mint of Guanaxuato. Stamp of 1825, 1826, 1827, 1828, 1829. (a.)

Weight, $"1.004=414.15 grs.=26.83 grms.
Fineness, 899—1000ths. Hort.
Value, $1.002=4*s.* 1.4*d.*=5.35 fr.

For Counterfeits, see Nos. 283 to 285, inclusive.

No. 141. ***Mexican Dollar.***

Mint of Guanaxuato. Stamp of 1828, in part. (b.)

Weight, $"1.010.=417 grs.=27.02 grms.
Fineness, 894—1000ths. Hort.
Value, $1.003=4*s.* 1.4*d.*=5.35 fr.

No. 142. ***Mexican Dollar.***

Mint of Guanaxuato. Stamp of 1829, in part. (c.)

Weight, $"1.000=412.50 grs.=26.726 grms.
Fineness, 893—1000ths. Hort.
Value, $0.992=4*s.* 0.9*d.*=5.30 fr.

No. 143. ***Mexican Dollar.***

Mint of Guanaxuato. Stamp of 1825 to 1829. (d.)

Weight, $"1.004=414.15 grs.=**26.83 grms.**

Fineness, 899—1000ths. Hort. Value, **$1.002=4***s.* 1.4*d.*=**5.35** fr.

No. 144. ***Mexican Dollar.***

Mint of Guanaxuato. Stamp of 1835. (a.)

For Weight, Fineness and Value, see stamp of 1830 to 1843, (c.) No. 146.

For Counterfeits, see Nos. 286 to 345 inclusive.

No. 145. ***Mexican Dollar.***

Mint of Guanaxuato. Stamp of 1836. (b.)

For Weight, Fineness and Value, see stamp of 1830 to 1843.

(c.) No. 146.

These dies, stolen perhaps from the mint, seem to have been used in the coinage of **debased metal.** Vide Nos, 324, 334, 335, 345. For Counterfeits, see Nos. 291 to **345 inclusive**

No. 146. ***Mexican Dollar.***

Mint of Guanaxuato. Stamp of 1830 to 1843. (c.)

Weight, $"1.011=417 grs.=27.02 grms.

Fineness, 896—1000ths, average. Value, $1.006=4*s.* 1.5*d.*=5.37 fr.

For Counterfeits, see Nos. 286 to 345, inclusive.

No. 147. ***Mexican Dollar.***

Mint of Guanaxuato. Stamp of 1843, (in part,) 1844. (a.)

Weight $"1.011=417 grs.=27.02 grms.

Fineness, near 899—1000ths. Value, $1.010=4*s.* 1.8*d.*=5.39 fr.

No. 148. ***Mexican Dollar.***

Mint of Guanaxuato. Stamp of 1844. (b.)

Weight, $"1.011=417 grs.=27.02 grms.

Fineness, 899—1000ths. Hort. Value, $1.010=4*s.* 1.8*d.*=5.39 fr.

For Counterfeit, see No. 346.

GENUINE MEXICAN DOLLARS.
Mint of Durango. Mint Mark D°

No. 149. ***Hook-Neck Dollar.*** Mint of Durango.
Weight, $''1.000.=412.50 grs.=26.726 grms.
Fineness, 900—1000ths.
Value, $1.000=4*s.* 1.3*d.*=5.34 fr.

No. 150. ***Hook-Neck Dollar.*** Mint of Durango.
Weight, $''1.000=412.50 grs.=26.726 grms.
Fineness, 901—1000ths.
Value, $1.001=4*s.* 1.3*d.*=5.34 fr.

No. 151. ***Hook-Neck Dollar.*** Mint of Durango.
Weight, $''1.000=412.50 grs.=26.726 grms.
Fineness, 900—1000ths.
Value, $1.000=4*s.* 1.3*d.*=5.34 fr.

No. 152. ***Mexican Dollar.***

Mint of Durango. Stamp of 1825. (a.)

Weight, $"1.000=412.50 grs.=26.726 grms.
Fineness, 897—100ths. Hort.
Value, $0.997=4*s.* 1.2*d.*=5.33 fr.

No. 153. ***Mexican Dollar.***

Mint of Durango. Stamp of 1825. (b.)

Weight, $"0.980=404.25 grs.=26.19 grms.
Fineness, 897—1000ths.
Value, $0.976=4*s.* 0.1*d.*=5.21 fr.

No. 154. ***Mexican Dollar.***

Mint of Durango. Stamp of 1825. (c.)

Weight, $"1.000=412.50 grs.=26.72 grms.
Fineness, 900—1000ths. Hort. Value, $1.000=4*s.* 1.3*d.*=5.34 fr.

No. 155. ***Mexican Dollar.***

Mint of Durango. Stamp of 1826, 1827, 1828.

Weight, $"1.011.=417 grs.=27.02 grms.
Fineness, 900—1000ths.
Value, $1.011=4*s*. 1.8*d*.=5.39 fr.

For Counterfeits, see Nos. 350 to 355, inclusive.

No. 156. ***Mexican Dollar.***

Mint of Durango. 1829, in part.

Weight, $"1.007=415,38 grs.=**26.90** grms.
Fineness, 900—1000ths. Value, **$1.007=4*s*.1.6*d*.=5.37** fr.

No. 157. ***Mexican Dollar.***

Mint of Durango. Stamp of 1829, 1830, 1831.

Weight, $"1.007=415.38 grs=**26.90** grms.
Fineness, 900—1000ths. Value, **$1.007=4*s*. 1.6*d*.=5.37** fr.

9 For Counterfeits, see Nos. 356 to 364, inclusive.

No. 158. ***Mexican Dollar.***

Mint of Durango. Stamp of 1832, in part.

Weight, **$"1.040.** Av. weight, **$"1.011=417** grs.=**27.02** grms.

Fineness, 901—1000ths. H o r t. Value, **$1.012=4*s*. 1.8*d*.=5.39 fr.**

For Counterfeits, see Nos. 365, 366.

No. 159. ***Mexican Dollar.***

Mint of Durango. Stamp of 1832, 1833, 1834.

Weight, **$"1.007=415.38** grs.=**26.90** grms.

Fineness, **900—1000**ths. Value, **$1.007=4*s*. 1.6*d*.=5.37** fr.

These dies seem to have been used in stamping base money. Vide Nos. 365, 371, 373 For Counterfeits, see Nos. 365 to 373, inclusive.

No. 160. ***Mexican Dollar.***

Mint of Durango. Stamp of 1835, 1836, 1837, 1838.

Weight, $"1.011=417 grs.=**27.02** grms.

Fineness, 902—1000ths. E c k f e l d t & D u b o i s.

Value, **$1.013=4*s*.** 1.8*d* =5 40 fr.

These dies seem to have been impressed, also, upon debased metal. Vide No. 374.

For Counterfeits, see Nos. 373, 375, 379, 381.

No. 161. ***Mexican Dollar.***

Mint of Durango. Stamp of 1839, 1840, 1841, 1842.

Weight, $ 1.011=417 grs.=**27.02** grms.

Fineness, 900—1000ths. Hort. Value, **$1.011=4***s.* 1.8*d.*=**5.39** fr.

For Counterfeits, see Nos. 376, to 381, inclusive.

No. 162. ***Mexican Dollar.***

Mint of Durango. Stamp of 1842, (in part,) 1843, 1844.

Weight, $ 1.011=417 grs.=**27.02** grms.

Fineness, 900—1000ths. Hort. Value, **$1.011.=4***s.* 1.8*d.*=**5.39** fr.

GENUINE MEXICAN DOLLARS.

Mint of San Luis Potosi. Mint Mark, Pᴵ

No. 163. ***Mexican Dollar.*** Mint of Potosi,

Weight, $ 1.000=412.5 grs.=**26.72** grms.

Fineness, 900—1000ths. Value, **$1.000=4***s.* 1.3*d.*=**5.34** fr.

Stamp of 1827. For Counterfeit, see No. 384.

No. 164. ***Mexican Dollar.***

Mint of Potosi.

Weight, $"1.008=415.80 grs.=26.936 grms.
Fineness, 900—1000ths. Value, $1.008=4*s.* 1.7*d.*=5.38 fr.

Dollars of this stamp bear date 1829, 1830, 1831, 1832.

For Counterfeits, see Nos. 385 to 387, inclusive.

No. 165. ***Mexican Dollar.***

Mint of Potosi.

Weight, $"1.010=416.26 grs.=26.993 grms.
Fineness, 900—1000ths.
Value, $1.010=4*s.* 1.8*d.*=5.39 fr.

Stamp of 1833.

No. 166. ***Mexican Dollar.***

Mint of Potosi.

Weight, $"1.008=415.80 grs.=26.936 grms.
Fineness, 900—1000ths. Value, $1.08=4*s.* 1.7*d*=5.38 fr.

Stamp of 1834. For Counterfeit, see No. 388.

No. 167. ***Mexican Dollar.***

Mint of Potosi. Stamp of 1835, 1836, 1837, 1838, 1839.

Weight, $"1.010=416.26 grs.=**26.993** grms.
Fineness, 901—1000ths. Eckfeldt & Dubois.
Value, $1.011=4*s.* 1.8*d.*=5.39 fr.

For Counterfeits, see Nos. 389, to 392, inclusive.

No. 168. ***Mexican Dollar.***

Mint of Potosi. Stamp of 1840, 1841.

Weight, $"1.011=417 grs.=**27.02** grms.
Fineness, 901—1000ths. Value, **$1.012=4***s.* 1.8*d.*=**5.40** fr.

No. 169. ***Mexican Dollar.***

Mint of Potosi. Stamp of 1842, 1843, 1844, (a.)

Weight, $"1.011=417 grs.=**27.02** grms.
Fineness, 901—1000ths. Value, **$1.012=4***s.* 1.8*d.*=**5.40** fr.

For Counterfeits, see Nos. 393, 394.

No. 170. ***Mexican Dollar.***

Mint of Potosi. Stamp of 1844. (b.)

Weight, $"1.011=417 grs.=27.02 grms.
Fineness, 901—1000ths. Value, $1.012=4*s.* 1.8*d.*=5.40 fr.

For Counterfeit, see No. 395.

GENUINE MEXICAN DOLLARS.
Mint of Chihuahua. Mint Mark, C^A^

No. 171. ***Mexican Dollar.***

Mint of Chihuahua. Stamp of 1832.

Weight, $"1.010=416.26 grs.=26.993 grms.
Fineness, 899—1000ths. Value, $1.009=4*s.* 1.7*d.*=5.38 fr.

No. 172. ***Mexican Dollar.***

Weight, $"1.011=417 grs.=27.02 grms.
Fineness, 898—1000ths. Value, $1.008=4*s.* 1.7*d.*=5.38 fr.

No. 173. ***Mexican Dollar.***

Mint of Chihuahua. Stamp of 1834, (in part,) 1835, 1836.

Weight, $"1.011=417 grs.=27.02 grms.
Fineness, 898—1000ths.
Value, $1.008=4*s.* 1.7*d.*=5.38 fr.

No. 174. ***Mexican Dollar.***

Mint of Chihuahua. Stamp of 1837, 1838.

Weight, $"1.011=417 grs.=27.02 grms.
Fineness, 898—1000ths.
Value, $1.008=4*s.* 1.7*d.*=5.38 fr.

No. 175. ***Mexican Dollar.***

Mint of Chihuahua. Stamp of 1840. (a.)

Weight, $"1.011=417 grs.=27.02 grms.
Fineness, 907—1000ths. Eckfeldt & Dubois.
Value, $1.019=4*s.* 2.2*d.*=5.44 fr.

No. 176. ***Mexican Dollar.***

Mint of Chihuahua. Stamp of 1840. (b.)

Weight, **$"1.010=416.26** grs.=**26.993** grms.

Fineness, **900—1000**ths. Value, **$**1.010=**4***s.* **1.8***d.*=**5.39** fr.

Weight very variable.

No. 177. ***Mexican Dollar.***

Mint of Chihuahua. Stamp of 1841, 1842, 1843.

Weight, **$"1.010=416.26** grs.=**26.993** grms.

Fineness, **900—1000**ths. Value, **$**1.010=**4***s.* **1.8***d.*=**5.39** fr.

No. 178. ***Mexican Dollar.***

Mint of Chihuahua. Stamp of 1844, **nearly same as 1843.**

Weight, **$"1.010=416.26** grs.=**26.993** grms.

Fineness 900—1000ths. Value, **$1.010=4***s.* **1.8***d.*=**5.39** fr.

GENUINE MEXICAN DOLLARS.
Mint of Guadalaxara. Mint Mark G^A

No. 179. ***Mexican Dollar.***

Mint of Guadalaxara. Stamp of 1825 to 1839, inclusive. (a.)

Weight, $"1.011=417 grs.=27.02 grms.

Fineness, 865—1000ths, av. Hort. Value, $0.971=3*s*. 11.8*d*.=5.18 fr.

The title varies from 840 to 895—1000ths. Eckfeldt & Dubois.

No. 180. ***Mexican Dollar.***

Mint of Guadalaxara. Stamp of 1825 to 1839. (b.)

Weight, $"1.011=417 grs.=27.02 grms.

Fineness, 865—1000ths, av. Hort. Value, $0.971=3*s*. 11.8*d*.=5.18 fr.

The fineness varies from 840 to 895—1000ths. Eckfeldt & Dubois.

Vide No. 398, a genuine stamp still more debased. For Counterfeits, see Nos. 396 to 398, inclusive.

No. 181. ***Mexican Dollar.***

Mint of Guadalaxara. Stamp of 1840, 1841, 1842, 1843, 1844.

Weight, $"1.011=417 grs.=27.02 grms.

Fineness, 900—1000ths. Hort. Value, $1.011=4*s*. 1.8*d*.=5.39 fr.

10 For Counterfeits, see Nos. 399, 400.

GENUINE MEXICAN DOLLAR.
Mint Mark, H°

No. 182. ***Mexican Dollar.***

Mint mark, H° 1835.

Weight, $\$^{wt}$1.010=417 grs.=27.02 grms.

Fineness, probably near 896=1000ths.

Value, $1.005=4*s.* 1.5*d.*=5.37 fr.

This coin must be rare, for I have met with but one, of which the above is a fac-simile.

COUNTERFEIT MEXICAN DOLLARS.

Mexican Dollars make up a principal part of the specie circulation of this country. Of these, as generally met with, about one in one hundred is counterfeit, and sometimes the proportion is very much greater. The great number of different stamps borne by the good Mexican Dollars, renders the detection of the bad ones, ordinarily, rather difficult. I am confident that the plan adopted in this work, will effectually aid in detecting nine counteifeits out of ten, as they are usually met with.

It will be seen that following the fac-simile of most of the counterfeits here given, are remarks on points of difference, as compared with the genuine coin. These remarks, usually very brief, might have been much more extended; but the extension I have not thought desirable, as a simple inspection and comparison of the fac-similes, will readily suggest many other points of difference to the observer. A pair of dividers for nicely measuring distances will be found of great use in these matters.

COUNTERFEIT MEXICAN DOLLARS.

Mint of Mexico. Mint Mark, M̊.

No. 183. ***Counterfeit Iturbide Dollar*, 1822 ? (a.)**

Weight, $\$$"0.880. Fineness, near 100—1000ths. Value, $\$$0.097.

Compare with No. 122. *Obverse*, head too large, neck too short. *Reverse*, dexter wing too straight and small.

No. 184. ***Counterfeit*, *Iturbide*, 1822. (b.)**

Weight, $\$$"0.990. Fineness, near 650—1000ths. Value, $\$$0.715.

Compare with No. 122. *Obverse*, hair wiry, lower part of the bust large. *Reverse*, cactus large, lettering imperfect.

No. 185. ***Counterfeit*, *Iturbide*, 1822. (c.)**

Weight, $\$$"1.010. Fineness, near 650—1000ths. Value, $\$$0.729.

Compare with No. 122. *Obverse*, superior part of the head large, lettering imperfect. *Reverse*, sinister wing large.

No. 186. ***Counterfeit, Iturbide,* 1823.**

Weight, $"1.030. Fineness, near 600—1000ths. Value, $0.686.

Compare with No. 122. *Obverse*, neck and lower part of the bust small, head imperfect. *Reverse*, cactus large.

No. 187. ***Counterfeit, Mexico,* 1824.** (a.)

Weight, $"1.020. Fineness, near 810—1000ths. Value, $0.918.

Compare with No. 127. *Obverse*, M, in the mint mark, too large. *Reverse*, leaves of the dexter vine too deeply notched.

No. 188. ***Counterfeit, Mexico,* 1824.** (b.)

Weight, $0.970. Fineness, near 755—1000ths. Value, 0.812.

Compare with Nos. 125, 126. Rays imperfect, lettering imperfect.

No. 189. ***Counterfeit, Mexico,* 1824.** (c.)
Weight, $1.000. Fineness, near 600—1000ths. Value, $0.666:
Compare with No. 127. *Obverse*, **M after the date too short and broad.** ***Reverse*, dexter leaves too deeply notched, snake's head too far from the eagle's head.**

No. 190. ***Counterfeit, Mexico,* 1824.** (d.)
Weight, $1.000. Fineness, 775—1000ths. Hort. Value, $0.861.
Compare with No. 127. Engraving of the plumage of the eagle too coarse, cactus leaves too large.

No. 191. ***Counterfeit, Mexico,* 1824.** (e.)
Weight, $0.970. Fineness, 755—1000ths. Hort.
Value, $0.812.
Compare with Nos. 125, 126. Rays imperfect, each having a raised line in the margin.

No. 192. ***Counterfeit, Mexico,* 1824.** (f.)

Weight, $"1.05. Fineness, near 760—1000ths. Value, $0.886.

Compare with Nos. 125, 126. *Obverse*, D. and G. too large.

No. 193. ***Counterfeit, Mexico,* 1824.** (g.)

Weight, $"1.000. Fineness, near 685—1000ths.. Value, $0.761.

Compare with Nos. 125, 126. Lettering small and imperfect, rays from the liberty cap different.

No. 194. ***Counterfeit, Mexico,* 1827.** (a.)

Weight, $"0.970. Fineness, 520—1000ths. Hort. Value, $0.560.

Compare with No. 128. Snake's neck irregularly crooked.

No. 195. ***Counterfeit, Mexico,* 1827.** (b.)
Weight, $"0.960. Fineness, near 630—1000ths. Value, $0.672.
Compare with No. 128. *Reverse*, dexter vine in the legend too coarse and rigid, sea too broad, snake's head and neck too much elevated from eagle's head.

No. 196. ***Mexico, Counterfeit,* 1829.**
Weight, $"0.860. Fineness, 250—1000ths. Hort. Value, $0.238.
Compare with No. 128. Leaves of the vines and cactus too small, snake's neck too slender.

No. 197. ***Counterfeit, Mexico,* 1830.** (a.)
Weight, $"0.980. Fineness, 514—1000ths. Hort. Value, $0.559.
Compare with Nos. 128, 129. Dexter leaves in the legend too much crowded, snake's neck awry.

No. 198. ***Counterfeit, Mexico,*** **1830.** (b.)

Weight, $"0.870. Fineness, 412—1000ths. Hort. Value, $0.398.

Compare with Nos. 124, 129. Cactus leaves too confluent, sea coarsely made.

No. 199. ***Counterfeit, Mexico,*** **1830.** (c.)

Weight, $"0.870. Fineness, near 200—1000ths. Value, 0.193.

Compare with Nos. 128, 129. Snake's neck too suddenly and irregularly crooked.

No. 200. ***Counterfeit, Mexico,*** **1833.** (a.)

Weight, $"1.050. Fineness, 655—1000ths. Hort. Value, $0.764.

Compare with Nos. 128, 129. Eagle's neck too small, letters in Republica too small, and very imperfect, snake's neck clumsy.

No. 201. ***Counterfeit Mexico*, 1833.** (b.)

Weight, $"0.980. Fineness, 750—1000ths. Hort.
Value, 0.816

Compare with Nos. 128, 129. **Eagles neck too small, and sinister wing too small next the body.**

No. 202. ***Counterfeit, Mexico*, 1834.**

Weight, $"0.960. Fineness, near 400—1000ths. Value, $0.426.

Compare with Nos. 128, 129. **Eagle too small, snake's neck too slender and crooked.**

No. 203. ***Counterfeit, Mexico*, 1835.** (a.)

Weight, $"0.930. Fineness, near 540—1000ths. **Value, $0.558.**

Compare with Nos. 128, 129. **Eagle's beak too short.**

No. 204. ***Counterfeit, Mexico,* 1835.** (b.)

Weight, $"1.010. Fineness, near 630—1000ths. Value, $0.707.

Compare with Nos. 128, 129. Snake's body too slender near the eagle's neck, leaves too large.

No. 205. ***Counterfeit, Mexico,* 1835** (c.)

Weight, $"1.030. Fineness, near 670—1000ths. Value, **$0.766.**

Compare with Nos. 128, 129. Eagle's wings too small.

No. 206. ***Counterfeit, Mexico,* 1836.** (a.)

Weight, $"0.940. Fineness, 650—1000ths. **H o r t.**

Value, $0.679.

Compare with No. 129. Lettering **too large.**

No. 207. ***Counterfeit, Mexico,* 1836.** (b.)
Weight, $"1.010. Fineness, 628—1000ths. H o r t. Value, $0.704.
Compare with No. 129. M too big after the date. Leaves in the legend too large.

No. 208. ***Counterfeit, Mexico,* 1836.** (c).
Weight, $"0.990. Fineness, 285—1000ths. H o r t. Value, $0.313.
Compare with No. 129. Admirably executed. The o over the M is too distinct. The sea is rather too narrow, and the cactus leaves differ in relative situation and direction slightly from those in the genuine coin.

No. 209. ***Counterfeit, Mexico,* 1836.** (d.)
Weight, $"0.990. Fineness, 285—1000ths. H o r t. Value, $0.313.
An assay piece has been cut from this coin. Compare with No. 129. Eagle's head too big.

No. 210. ***Counterfeit, Mexico,* 1838.**

Appears to have been cast in a mould.

Weight, \$"0.900. Fineness, near 370—1000ths. Value, **\$0.370.**

Compare with No. 129. Impression blunt.

No. 211. ***Counterfeit, Mexico,* 1839.**

Weight, \$"0.970. Fineness, 728—1000ths. Hort. Value, \$0.784.

Compare with No. 129. Snake's head and neck too large.

No. 212. ***Counterfeit, Mexico,* 1842.**

Weight, \$"0.950. Fineness, near 300—1000ths. Value, \$0.316.

Compare with No. 129. Snake's head too much elongated and elevated.

COUNTERFEIT MEXICAN DOLLARS.
Mint of Zacatecas. Mint Mark, Z^s

No. 213. ***Counterfeit, Zacatecas,*** **1825.**
Weight, $"0.800. Fineness, near 450—1000ths. Value, $0.400.
A fair imitation, not easily distinguished from the genuine stamp, No. 134. *Obverse*, figures of the date rather too small. *Reverse*, cactus leaves too large.

No. 214. ***Counterfeit, Zacatecas,*** 1826.
Weight, $"0.770. Fineness, 130—1000ths. Hort. Value, $0.111.
Compare with No. 135. Wings and cactus leaves too large.

No. 215. ***Counterfeit, Zacatecas,*** **1828.** (a.)
Weight, $"1.020. Fineness, 280—1000ths. Hort. Value, $0.317.
Compare with No. 136. Wings too large, lettering very imperfect.

No. 216. ***Counterfeit, Zacatecas,* 1828.** (b.)
Weight, $1.060. Fineness, 260—1000ths. Hort. Value, $0.306.
Compare with No. 136. Snake's body too large. Letters of Re, ublica irregular.

No. 217. ***Counterfeit, Zacatecas,* 1828.** (c.)
Weight, $0.970. Fineness, 194—1000ths. Hort. Value, $0.205.
Compare with No. 136. Eagle's beak and snake's neck too long,

---

No. 218. ***Counterfeit, Zacatecas,* 1829.** (a.)
Weight, $0.950. Fineness, near 180—1000ths. Value, $0.190.
Compare with No. 136. Snake's neck too long and large.

No. 219. ***Counterfeit, Zacatecas,*** **1829.** (b.)
Weight, $"0.800. Fineness, 300—1000ths. Hort. Value, $0.266.
Compare with No. 136. Snake's neck too long and large, ground too high.

No .220. ***Counterfeit, Zacatecas,*** **1829.** (c.)
Weight, $"0.870. Fineness, near 54—1000ths. Value, $0.052.
Compare with No. 136. Snake's neck too long.

No. 221. ***Counterfeit, Zacatecas,*** **1829.** (d.)
Weight, $"0.930. Fineness, near 63—1000ths. Value, $0.065.
Compare with No. 136. Snake's neck too long, ground too low.

No. 222. ***Counterfeit, Zacatecas,* 1829.** (e.)

Weight, $"0. 900. Fineness, near 375—1000ths. **Value, $0.375.**
Compare with No. 136. Snake's neck too long, body too large.

No. 223. ***Counterfeit, Zacatecas,* 1832.** (a.)

Weight, $"0.930. Fineness, 370—1000ths. Hort. Value, $0.382.
Compare with No. 136. Stamp admirably imitated, or perhaps genuine, but the snake's neck seems a little too far from the eagle's head. **This counterfeit is very abundant, bearing dates** 1829, 1830, 1832, 1833.

No. 224. ***Counterfeit, Zacatecas,* 1832.** (b.)

Weight, $" 1.000. Fineness, near 360—1000ths. Value, $0.400.
Compare with No. 136. Snake's body too straight.

No. 225. ***Counterfeit, Zaca ecas*, 1832.** (c.)

Weight, $"0.850. Fineness, 153—1000ths. H o r t. Value, **$0.144.**

Compare with No. 136. Liberty cap too large, rays too numerous.

No. 226. ***Counterfeit, Zacatecas*, 1833.** (a.)

Weight, $"0.880. Fineness, 500—1000ths. H o r t. Value, **$0.488.**

Compare with No. 136. Cap too large, rays too numerous.

No. 227. ***Counterfeit, Zacatecas*, 1833.** (b.)

Weight, $"0.900. Fineness, 396—1000ths. H o r t. Value, **$0.396.**

12 Compare with No. 136. Snake's neck too long.

No. 228. ***Counterfeit, Zacatecas,* 1833.** (c.)
Weight, $\$$"1.000. Fineness, 264—1000ths. Value, **$\$$0.293.**
The assay of three individual coins, gave 214, 264, 269—1000ths. Compare with No. 136. Lettering coarse, snake's nose too straight.

No. 229. ***Counterfeit, Zacatecas,* 1833.** (d.)
Weight, $\$$"0.850. Fineness, near 630—1000ths. Value, **$\$$0.595.**
Compare with No. 136. Snake's neck too high above the eagle's head.

No. 230. ***Counterfeit, Zacatecas,* 1833.** (e.)
Weight, $\$$"0.930. Fineness, 212—1000ths. Value, $\$$0.219.
Compare with No. 136. Rays below the cap too large and irregularly divergent.

No. 231. ***Counterfeit, Zacatecas,* 1833.** (f.)

Weight, $"0.900. Fineness, near 126—1000ths. Value, $0.126.

Compare with No. 136. Eagle's neck too small, snake's neck too short.

No. 232. ***Counterfeit, Zacatecas,* 1833.** (g.)

Weight, $"0.980. Fineness, near 72—1000ths. Value, $0.078.

Compare with No. 136. Lettering irregular, snake's head rather too large.

No. 233. ***Counterfeit, Zacatecas,* 1834.** (a.)

Weight, $"1.000. Fineness, 250—1000ths. Hort. Value, $0.277.

Compare with No. 136. Snake's head too small, plumage of the eagle too hairy.

No. 234. ***Counterfeit, Zacatecas,*** **1834.** (b.)
Weight, $"1.070. Fineness, near 9—1000ths. Value, **$0.010.**
Copper washed with silver. The date 1836 observed, same stamp. Compare with No. 136. Snake's body too large.

No. 235. ***Counterfeit, Zacatecas,*** **1834.** (c.)
Weight, $"0.800. Fineness, near **300—1000ths.** Value, **$0.266.**
Compare with No. 136. An excellent imitation. *Obverse,* **Z rather too large and M rather too small.**

No. 236. ***Counterfeit, Zacatecas,*** **1834.** (d.)
Weight, $"0.960. Fineness, near **345—1000ths.** Value, **$0.368.**
Compare with No. 136. Snake's body too crooked.

No. 237. ***Counterfeit, Zacatecas,*** **1834.** (e.)

Weight, $"1.000. Fineness, near 630—1000ths. Value, $0.700.

Compare with No. 156. Eagle's body too small.

No. 238. ***Counterfeit, Zacatecas,*** **1835.** (a.)

Weight, $"0.900. Fineness, 5—1000ths. Hort. Value $0.005.

Copper washed or plated with silver. A very common counterfeit. Compare with **No. 136.** Snake's body too large.

No. 239. ***Counterfeit, Zacatecas,*** **1835.** (b.)

Weight, $"0.900. Fineness, near 18—1000ths. Value, 0.18.

Copper washed with silver. Compare with No. 136. Snake's neck not enough **curved.**

No. 240. ***Counterfeit, Zacatecas,*** **1835.** (c.)

Weight, $"0.930. Fineness, near 9—1000ths. Value, $0.009.

Copper washed with silver. Compare with No. 136. Dexter wing too near the body.

No. 241. ***Counterfeit, Zacatecas,*** **1835.** (d.)

Weight, $"1.000. Fineness, 632—1000ths. Hort. Value, $0.700.

Compare with No. 136. Wings too large.

No. 242. ***Counterfeit, Zacatecas,*** **1835.** (e.)

Weight, $"0.820. Fineness, 420—1000ths. Hort. Value, $0.382.

Compare with No. 136. Neck of the snake too straight, large and long.

No. 243. ***Counterfeit, Zacatecas,* 1835.** (f.)
Weight, $"0.950. Fineness, 392—1000ths. H o r t. Value, $0.413.
Compare with No. 136. Eagle's head too small.

No. 244. ***Counterfeit, Zacatecas,* 1835.** (g.)
Weight, $"1.060. Fineness, 232—1000ths. H o r t. Value, $0.273
Compare with No. 136. Snake irregularly crooked.

No. 245. ***Counterfeit, Zacatecas,* 1835.** (h.)
Weight, $"0.950. Fineness, 232—1000ths. H o r t. Value, $0.244.
Compare with No. 136. Snake's body too small.

No. 246. ***Counterfeit, Zacatecas,*** **1835.** (i.)
Weight, $"0.910.
Fineness, 330—1000ths, average. H o r t. Value, **$0.344.**
Compare with No. 136. Snake's neck too short.

No. 247. ***Counterfeit, Zacatecas,*** **1836.** (a.)
Weight, $"0.850. Fineness, 192—1000ths. H o r t. **Value, $0.181.**
The same stamp also bears date 1833. Very common. **Compare with No. 137.**
Lettering irregular.

No. 248. ***Counterfeit, Zacatecas,*** **1836.** (b.)
Weight, $"0.890. Fineness, 182—1000ths. H o r t. **Value, $0.179.**
Compare with No. 137. **This excellent imitation may be recognized by the smallness of the letters and figures on the cap side.**

No. 249. ***Counterfeit, Zacatecas,*** **1836.** (c.)

Weight, $"0.800. Fineness, near 18—1000ths. Value, **$0.016.**

Compare with No. 137. Cactus leaves too confluent.

No. 250. ***Counterfeit, Zacatecas,*** **1836.** (d.)

Weight, $"0.830. Fineness, near 18—1000ths. Value, **$0.016.**

Compare with No. 137. Snake's neck too long.

No. 251. ***Counterfeit, Zacatecas,*** **1836.** (e.)

Weight, $"1.030. Fineness, 125—1000ths. Hort. Value, **$0.143.**

13 Compare with No. 137. Leaves too small.

No. 252. ***Counterfeit, Zacatecas,* 1836.** (f.)
Weight, $"0.900. Fineness, 54—1000ths. H o r t. Value, $0.054.
Compare with No. 137. **Snake's neck irregularly curved.**

No. 253. ***Counterfeit, Zacatecas,* 1836.** (g.)
Weight, $"1.010. Fineness, near 207—1000ths. Value, $0.232.
Compare with No. 137. **Snake's neck irregularly curved.**

No. 254. ***Counterfeit, Zacatecas,* 1836.** (h.)
Weight, $"0.790. Fineness, near 720—1000ths. Value, $0.632.
Appears to have been cast. Compare with No. 137. **Impression blunt.**

No. 255. ***Counterfeit, Zacatecas*, 1836.** (i.)

Weight, $"0.910. Fineness, 180—1000ths. Hort. Value, $0.182.

Compare with No. 137. Snake's head too large.

No. 256. ***Counterfeit, Zacatecas*, 1837.** (a.)

Weight, $"0.850. Fineness, 55—1000ths. Hort. Value, $0.051.

Compare with No. 137. Cactus leaves distinct, snake's neck not enough curved.

No. 257. ***Counterfeit, Zacatecas*, 1837,** (b.)

Weight, $"0.850. Fineness, 5—1000ths. Hort. Value, $0.005.

Compare with No. 137. Snake's neck not enough curved.

No. 258. ***Counterfeit, Zacatecas*, 1837.** (c.)

Weight, $\$^{w}$1.000. Fineness, 40—1000ths. Hort. Value, **\$0.044.**

Compare with No. 137. Snake's neck not enough curved.

No. 259. ***Counterfeit, Zacatecas*, 1837.** (d.)

Weight, $\$^{w}$0.980. Fineness, near 300—1000ths. Value, **\$0.326.**

Compare with No. 137. Snake's neck too straight.

No. 260. ***Counterfeit, Zacatecas*, 1838.** (a.)

Weight, $\$^{w}$0.710. Fineness, 450—1000ths. Hort. Value, **\$0.355.**

Compare with No. 137. Snake's neck too large and straight.

No. 261. ***Counterfeit, Zacatecas,*** **1838.** (b.)
Weight, $"0.960. Fineness, near 27—1000ths. Value, $0.028.
Compare with No. 137. Eagle's head defective.

No. 262. ***Counterfeit, Zacatecas,*** **1839.** (a.)
Weight, $"0.810. Fineness, 44—1000ths. Hort. Value, $0.039.
Compare with No. 137. Lettering irregular, Z too narrow.

No. 263. ***Counterfeit, Zacatecas,*** **1839.** (b.)
Weight, $"1.020. Fineness, 30—1000ths. Hort. Value, $0.033.
Compare with No. 137. Snake's neck too straight.

No. 264. ***Counterfeit, Zacatecas,*** **1839.** (c.)

Weight, $"0.900. Fineness, near 270—1000ths.. **Value, $0.270.**

Compare with No. 137. **Snake's neck too straight.**

No. 265. ***Counterfeit, Zacatecas,*** **1839.** (d.

Weight, $"0.860. Fineness, near 162—1000ths. **Value, $0.154.**

Compare with No. 137. **Snake's neck too low.**

No. 266. ***Counterfeit, Zacatecas,*** **1840.** (a.)

Weight, $"0.950. Fineness, 333—1000ths. H o r t. **Value, $0.390.**

Compare with No. 137. **Snake's head too large.**

No. 267. ***Counterfeit Zacatecas*, 1840.** (b.)
Weight, $"0.880. Fineness, 48—1000ths. H o r t. Value, $0.047.
Compare with No. 137. Snake's neck too short.

No. 268. ***Counterfeit, Zacatecas*, 1840.** (c.)
Weight, $"0.950. Fineness, near 180—1000ths. Value, $0.190.
Compare with No. 137. Rays too compact, snake's neck too straight.

No. 269. ***Counterfeit, Zacatecas*, 1841.** (a.)
Weight, $"1.070. Fineness, 0—1000ths. Value, $0.000.
German silver. Compare with No. 137. Snake's neck too straight.

No. 270. ***Counterfeit, Zacatecas,*** **1841.** (b.)

Weight, $"0.870. Fineness, near 378—1000ths. Value, $0.365.

Compare with No. 137. A good imitation. Sinister vine leaves too large, snake's body rather large.

No. 271. ***Counterfeit, Zacatecas,*** **1841.** (c.)

Weight, $"1.000. Fineness, 450—1000ths. H o r t. Value, $0.500.

Compare with No. 137. Leaves too small. A most abundant counterfeit. A white alloy of silver and German silver.

No. 272. ***Counterfeit, Zacatecas,*** **1842.** (a.)

Weight, $"1.000. Fineness, 450—1000ths. Hort. Value, $0.500.

Abundant. Compare with No. 138. Rays irregular.

No. 273. ***Counterfeit, Zacatecas,* 1842.** (b.)
Weight, $"1.000. Fineness, 450—1000ths. H o r t. Value, $0.500.
Compare with No. 138. Rays irregular,

No. 274. ***Counterfeit, Zacatecas,* 1842.** (c.)
Weight, $"1.000. Fineness, near 150—1000ths. Value, $0.166.
Compare with No. 138. Wings too small.

No. 275. ***Counterfeit, Zacatecas,* 1842.** (d.)
Weight, $"0.890. Fineness, near 72—1000ths. Value, $0.071.
14 Compare with No. 138. Wings too small.

No. 276. ***Counterfeit, Zacatecas,* 1842.** (e.)
Weight, $"0.850. Fineness, near 20—1000ths. Value, **$0.020:**
Compare with No. 138. **Dexter vine stem too straight.**

No. 277. ***Counterfeit, Zacatecas,* 1842.** (f.)
Weight, $"0.950. Fineness, near 630—1000ths. Value, **$0.665.**
Compare with No. 138. **Dexter vine stem too straight.**

No. 278. ***Counterfeit, Zacatecas,* 1843.** (a.)
Weight, $"1.000. Fineness, 450—1000ths. Hort. **Value, $0.500.**
Abundant. Compare with No. 138. **Rays irregular.**

No. 279. ***Counterfeit, Zacatecas,* 1843.** (b.)

Weight, $"1.000. Fineness, **450—1000ths.** Hort. Value, **$0.500.**

Compare with No. 138. Rays irregular.

No. 280. ***Counterfeit, Zacatecas,* 1843.** (c.)

Weight, $"1.000. Fineness, **450—1000ths.** Hort. Value, **$0.500.**

Common. Compare with No. 138. Rays irregular.

No. 281. ***Counterfeit, Zacatecas,* 1843.** (d.)

Weight, $"0.910. Fineness, near **10—1000ths.** Value, **$0.010.**

Compare with No. 138. Inferior rays too long.

No. 282. ***Counterfeit, Zacatecas,*** **date effaced.**
Weight, $"1.010. Fineness, near 360—1000ths. Value, $0.404.
Compare with No. 136. Snake's head too large.

DEBASED AND COUNTERFEIT MEXICAN DOLLARS.
Mint of Guanaxuato. Mint Mark G°

No. 283. ***Counterfeit, Guanaxuato,*** **1828.**
Weight, $"0.910. Fineness, near 450—1000ths. Value, $0.455.
Compare with Nos. 140, 141. Snake's head too far from eagle's head.

No.284. ***Counterfeit, Guanaxuato,*** **1829.** (a.)
Weight, $"0.900. Fineness, 228—1000ths. Hort. Value, $0.228.
Compare with Nos. 140, 142, 143. Snake's neck too short, and too near the letter A.

No. 285. *Counterfeit, Guanaxuato,* 1829. (b.)
Weight, $"0.870. Fineness, near 90—1000ths. Value, $0.087.
Compare with Nos. 140, 142, 143. Sea too large, snake's head too large in relation to his neck.

No. 286. *Counterfeit, Guanaxuato,* 1830. (a.)
Weight, $"0.960. Fineness, near 720—1000ths. Value, $0.768.
Compare with No. 146. Leaves of the dexter vine too deeply notched. Snake's neck too high above the eagle's head.

No. 287. *Counterfeit, Guanaxuato,* 1830. (b.)
Weight, $"0.950. Fineness, near 75—1000ths. Value, $0.079.
Compare with No. 146. Snake's head too large, eagle's head too small.

No. 288. ***Counterfeit, Guanaxuato,* 1830.** (c.)
Weight, **$"1.000.** Fineness, near **270—1000ths.** Value, **$0.300.**
Compare with No. 146. Snake's head and neck too large.

No. 289. ***Counterfeit, Guanaxuato,* 1830.** (d.)
Weight, **$"0.950.** Fineness, near **720—1000ths.** Value, **$0.760.**
Compare with No. 146. Snake's head and neck too large.

No. 290. ***Counterfeit, Guanaxuato,* 1830.** (e.)
Weight, **$"1.010.** Fineness, near **330—1000ths.** Value, **$0.370.**
Compare with No. 146. Snake's neck curved too high from the eagle's head.

No. 291. ***Counterfeit, Guanaxuato,* 1831.** (a.
Weight, $"0.820. Fineness, 223—1000ths. Hort. Value, **$0.203.**
Compare with No. 146. Angle of the right wing with the body too sharp, left wing wrongly curved.

No. 292. ***Counterfeit, Guanaxuato,* 1831.** (b.)
Weight, $"0.950. Fineness, 410—1000ths. Hort. Value, **$0.432.**
Compare with No 146. Sea too large.

No. 293. ***Counterfeit, Guanaxuato,* 1831.** (c.)
Weight, $"0.900. Fineness, 217—1000ths. Hort. Value, $0.217.
Compare with No. 146. Vines very unlike 146. Eagle's plumage too fine, snake's neck wrongly curved.

No. 294. *Counterfeit, Guanaxuato,* 1831. (d.)
Weight, $"0.950. Fineness, near 450—1000ths. Value, **$0.47**
Compare with No. 146. Snake's neck too long.

No. 295. *Counterfeit Guanaxuato,* 1831. (e.)
* Weight, $"0.820. Fineness, near 36—1000ths. Value, **$0.328.**
Compare with No. 146. Leaves of the vines too large. Snake's head curved too much down.

No. 296. *Counterfeit, Guanaxuato,* 1831. (f.)
Weight, $"0.790. Fineness, near 270—1000ths. Value, **$0.237.**
Compare with No. 146. King die portions of the stamp, cap and rays, eagle and appurtenances, apparently genuine. M. J. too small.

No. 297. *Counterfeit, Guanaxuato,* 1831. (g.)

Weight, $"0.810. Fineness, **411—1000ths. Hort.** Value, **$0.369.**

Compare with No. 146. Snake's neck apparently broken.

No. 298. *Counterfeit, Guanaxuato,* 1831. (h.)

Weight, $"0.950. Fineness, near **450—1000ths.** Value, **$0.475.**

Compare with No. 146. Rays from the cap, and plumage of the eagle defective.

No. 299. *Counterfeit, Guanaxuato,* 1832. (a.)

Weight, $"0.960. Fineness, near **1—1000ths.** Value, **$0.001.**

Copper thinly washed over with silver. Compare with No. 146. Snake's body below the eagle's beak too small, and wrongly curved.

15

No. 300. ***Counterfeit, Guanaxuato,*** **1832.** (b.)
Weight, $"0.930. Fineness, near 360—1000ths. Value, $0.372.
A good imitation. Compare with No. 146. Cap rather too small, snake's nose rather too long.

No. 301. ***Counterfeit, Guanaxuato,*** **1832.** (c.)
Weight, $"1.070. Fineness, near 360—1000ths. Value, $0.428.
Compare with No. 146. Snake's head too high, and body too straight.

No. 302. ***Counterfeit, Guanaxuato,*** **1832.** (d.)——
Weight, $"0.810. Fineness, 257—1000ths. H o r t. Value, $0.231.
Compare with No. 146. Cap and rays, eagle and appurtenances, apparently genuine. M. J. too small.

No. 303. ***Counterfeit, Guanaxuato,* 1833.** (a.)
Weight, $"0.880. Fineness, near 10—1000ths. Value, $0.010.
Compare with No. 146. Rays and vines very unlike No. 146.

No. 304. ***Counterfeit, Guanaxuato,* 1833.** (b.)
Weight, $"0.800. Fineness, near 130—1000ths. Value $0.115.
Compare with No. 146. A good imitation. Left wing rather too small.

No. 305. ***Counterfeit, Guanaxuato,* 1833.** (c.)
Weight, $"1.070. Fineness, near 200—1000ths. Value, $0.237.
Compare with No. 146. Snake's neck too far from eagle's neck.

No. 306. *Counterfeit, Guanaxuato,* 1833. (d.)
Weight, $"1.030. Fineness, 40—1000ths. Hort. Value, **$0.045.**
Compare with No. 146. Plumage too fine.

No. 307. *Counterfeit, Guanaxuato,* 1833. (e.)
Weight, $"0.850. Fineness, near 18—1000ths. Value, **$0.017.**
Compare with No. 146. Snake's head too much elevated.

No. 308. *Counterfeit, Guanaxuato,* 1833. (f.)
Weight, $"0.910. Fineness, 602—1000ths. Hort. Value, **$0.608.**
Compare with No. 146. Snake's head too much elevated.

No. 309. ***Counterfeit, Guanaxuàto,* 1834.** (a.)

Weight, $\$^{w}$0.830. Fineness, near 126—1000ths. Value, $0.116.

Compare with No. 146. Snake's head rather too large, neck rather long, and too much curved down, cap and rays apparently perfect.

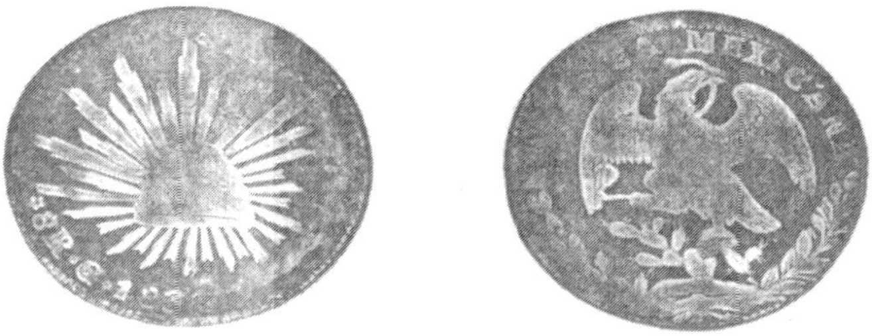

No. 310. ***Counterfeit, Guanaxuato,* 1834.** (b.)

Weight, $\$^{w}$1.030. Fineness, near 630—1000ths. Value, $0.721.

Compare with No. 146. Snake's head rather too large, cactus leaves different from 146.

No. 311. ***Counterfeit, Guanaxuato,* 1834.** (c.)

Weight, $\$^{w}$0.930. Fineness, near 18—1000ths. Value, $0.186.

Compare with No. 146. Eagle's head too small.

No. 312. *Counterfeit, Guanaxuato,* 1834. (d.)
Weight, $"0.830. Fineness, 87—1000ths. Hort. Value, $0.080.
Compare with No. 146. Snake's head rather too far from the eagle's head.

No. 313. *Counterfeit, Guanaxuato,* 1834. (e.)
Weight, $"1.030. Fineness, 40—1000ths. Hort. Value, $0.045.
Compare with No. 146. Plumage too fine, snake badly curved.

No. 314. *Counterfeit, Guanaxuato,* 1834. (f.)
Weight, $"0.920. Fineness, 170—1000ths. Value, $0.173.
Compare with No. 146. Snake's neck too short and too much curved.

No. 315. ***Counterfeit, Guanaxuato,* 1834.** (g.)
Weight, $"0.820. Fineness, 75—1000ths. Hort. Value, $0.068.
Compare with No. 146. Snake's head too large.

No. 316. ***Counterfeit, Guanaxuato,* 1834.** (h.)
Weight, $"0.900. Fineness, near 255—1000ths. Value, $0.255.
Compare with No. 146. Snake's head curved too much down.

No. 317. ***Counterfeit, Guanaxuato,* 1834.** (i.)
Weight, $"0.890. Fineness, near 360—1000ths. Value, $0.356.
Compare with No. 146. Eagle's beak too blunt, snake's neck too small.

No. 318. ***Counterfeit, Guanaxuato,* 1834.** (j.)
Weight, $"1.040. Fineness, near 430—1000ths. Value, **$0.496**.
Compare with No. 146. Eagle's wings too small.

No. 319. ***Counterfeit, Guanaxuato,* 1835.** (a.)
Weight, $"0.950. Fineness, 285—1000ths. H o r t. Value, **$0.300**.
Compare with No. 144. Snake's head too large.

No. 320. ***Counterfeit, Guanaxuato,* 1835.** (b.)
Weight, $"0.930. Fineness, 486—1000ths. H o r t. Value, **$0.479**.
Compare with No. 144. Plumage checkered, cactus leaves too small.

No. 321. ***Counterfeit, Guanaxuato,*** **1835.** (c.)
Weight, $"1.000. Fineness, near 140—1000ths. Value, $0.011.
Compare with No. 144. Snake's neck wrongly curved.

No. 322. ***Counterfeit, Guanaxuato,*** **1835.** (d.)
Weight, $"0.990. Fineness, near 630—1000ths. Value, $0.693.
Compare with No. 144. Snake's head too large. Eagle's plumage checkered.

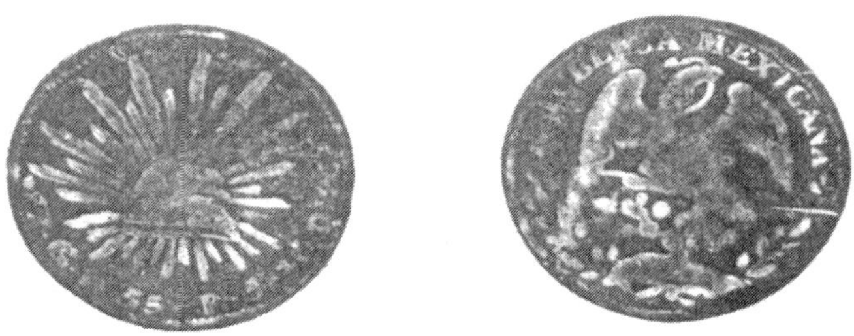

No. 323. ***Counterfeit, Guanaxuato,*** **1835.** (e.)
Weight, $"0.810. Fineness, near 15—1000ths. Value, $0.105.
Compare with No. 144. Impression dull.

16

No. 324. *Debased Dollar, Guanaxuato,* 1836. (a.)

Weight, $"0.980. Fineness, 466—1000ths. Hort. Value, $0.507.

Stamp genuine. Vide No. 145. The figure 6 in the date rather smaller and more inclined than in the good coins. The weight of these coins irregular, varying from $0.90 to $1.15.

No. 325. *Counterfeit, Guanaxuato,* 1836. (b.)

Weight, $"0.940. Fineness, 257—1000ths. Hort. Value, $0.268.

Compare with No. 145. Snake's head too near eagle's head.

No. 326. *Counterfeit, Guanaxuato,* 1836. (c.)

Weight, $"1.060. Fineness, 0—1000ths. Value, $0.000.

Made of copper. Compare with No. 145. Vine leaves too small.

No. 327. ***Counterfeit, Guanaxuato,* 1836.** (d.)
Weight, $"0.790. Fineness, near 9—1000ths. Value, **$0.008**:
Compare with No. 145. Snake's neck too short.

No. 328. ***Counterfeit, Guanaxuato,* 1836.** (e.)
Weight, $"0.910. Fineness, near **22**—1000ths. Value, **$0.022.**
Compare with No. 145. Snake's head too close to eagle's head.

No. 329. ***Counterfeit, Guanaxuato,* 1837.** (a.)
Weight, $"1.020. **Fineness, 718—1000ths.** H o r t . **Value, $0.814.**
Compare with No. 145. Snake's head curved down too much.

No. 330. *Counterfeit, Guanaxuato*, 1837. (b.)
Weight, $"0.950. Fineness, near 360—1000ths. Value, $0.380
Compare with No. 145. Leaves of right vine and cactus rather small.

No. 331. *Counterfeit, Guanaxuato*, 1837. (c.)
Weight, $"0.850. Fineness, near 90—1000ths. Value, $0.085.
An excellent imitation, Vide No. 145. Snake's head rather large, and rather too near the eagle's head.

No. 332. *Counterfeit, Guanaxuato*, 1837. (d.)
Weight, $"1.000. Fineness, 0—1000ths. Value, $0.000.
German silver. Compare with No. 145. Snake and eagle deformed.

No. 333. *Counterfeit, Guanaxuato,* 1837. (e.)

Weight, "$0.920. Fineness, 1—1000ths. Value, $0.001.

Brass washed with silver. Charles McDonald's coin. Compare with No. 145. Snake's head too large, rays defective.

No. 334. *Debased Dollar, Guanaxuato,* 1838. (a.)

Weight, $"0.950. Fineness, 457—1000ths. H o r t. Value, $0.482.

King die portions (the eagle, cap and appurtenances,) genuine stamp. Lettering in the legend more irregular than in the full standard coins. Vide No. 145.

No. 335. *Debased Dollar, Guanaxuato,* 1838. (b.)

Weight, $"0.950. Fineness, 477—1000ths. H o r t. Value, $0.503.

Stamp apparently like 1838, (a.) No. 334, but containing rather more silver as shown by assay. The letters are not as much raised in these as in the full standard coins.

No. 336. ***Counterfeit, Guanaxuato,* 1839.** (a.)
Weight, $"0.900. Fineness, near 90—1000ths. **Value, $0.090.**
Compare with No. 145. **Snake's body bows out too far from the eagle's neck.**

No. 337. ***Counterfeit, Guanaxuato,* 1839.** (b.)
Weight, $"0.950. Fineness, near 18—1000ths. **Value, $0.019.**
Compare with No. 145. **Plumage checkered with too much regularity.**

No. 338. ***Counterfeit, Guanaxuato,* 1839.** (c.)
Weight, $"0.730. Fineness, 451—1000ths. `Hort: **Value, $0.366.**
Compare with No. 145. **Eagle's head too small.**

No. 339. ***Counterfeit, Guanaxuato,*** **1839.** (d.)
Weight, $"0.940. Fineness, 37—1000ths. H o r t. Value, $0.038.
Compare with No. 145. Snake's head too large.

No. 340. ***Counterfeit, Guanaxuato,*** **1839.** (e.)
Weight, $"0.820. Fineness, near 18—1000ths. Value, $0.016.
Compare with Nos. 145. Snake's head too remote from eagle's head.

No. 341. ***Counterfeit, Guanaxuato,*** **1840.** (a.)
Weight, $"0.690. Fineness, near 3—1000ths. Value, $0.002.
Compare with No. 145. Eagle's head too small.

No. 342. ***Counterfeit, Guanaxuato,*** **1840.** (b.)
Weight, $"0.980. Fineness, near 540—1000ths. Value, $0.588.
Compare with No. 145. Snake's neck too near the eagle's head.

No. 343. ***Counterfeit, Guanaxuato,*** **1840.** (c.)
Weight, $"0.910. Fineness, near 630—1000ths. Value, $0.637.
Compare with No. 145. Snake's neck and body too large.

No. 344. ***Counterfeit, Guanaxuato,*** **1841.**
Weight, $"0.980. Fineness, near 90—1000ths. Value, $0.098.
Compare with No. 145. Snake's head too large.

No. 345. *Debased Dollar, Guanaxuato,* 1842.

Weight, $"0.910. Fineness, near 450—1000ths.. Value, $0.455.

Stamp apparently genuine. Compare with No. 145. The snake's neck and head seem rather too large.

No. 346. *Counterfeit, Guanaxuato,* 1844.

Weight, $"0.890. Fineness, near 5—1000ths. Value, $0.004.

Compare with No. 148. Snake's neck too short.

No. 347. *Counterfeit, Guanaxuato,* date obscure.

Weight, $"0.990. Fineness, near 450—1000ths. Value, $0.495.

No. 348. ***Counterfeit, Guanaxuato,*** **date effaced.**
Weight, $"1.000. Fineness, 270—1000ths. Value, $0.300

No. 349. ***Counterfeit, Guanaxuato,*** **date effaced.**
Weight, $"0.960. Fineness, near 18—1000ths. Value, $0.019.

DEBASED AND COUNTERFEIT MEXICAN DOLLARS.
Mint of Durango. Mint Mark, Dº

No. 350. ***Counterfeit, Durango,*** **1826.** (a.)
Weight, $"0.930. Fineness, 300—1000ths. H o r t. **Value, $0.310.**

Date of 1827 of this stamp observed. Also the date 1838. **Compare with No. 156.** Superior rays oblique.

No. 351. ***Counterfeit, Durango,* 1826.** (b.)

Same die as in 1826, (a.) but different value.

Weight, $"0.990. Fineness, 244—1000ths. H o r t. Value, $0.268.

Compare with No. 156. Superior rays oblique.

No. 352. ***Counterfeit, Durango,* 1826.** (c.)

Weight, $"0.970. Fineness, near 230—1000ths. Value $0.247.

Compare with No. 156. Eagle's head too large.

No. 353. ***Counterfeit, Durango,* 1827.**

Weight, $"0.850. Fineness, near 270—1000ths. Value $0.255.

Compare with No. 152. Leaves of left vine too long and large.

No. 354. *Counterfeit, Durango,* 1828. (a.)
Weight, $"0.910. Fineness, 446—1000ths. Hort. Value, $0.450.
Compare with No. 156. Eagle's neck too small.

No. 355. *Counterfeit, Durango,* 1828. (b.)
Weight, $"0.830. Fineness, near 200—1000ths. Value, $0.184.
Compare with No. 156. Snake wrongly curved.

No. 356. *Counterfeit, Durango,* 1829. (a.)
Weight, $"1.860. Fineness, 885—1000ths Hort. Value, $0.851.
Compare with No. 157. Snake's head too high.

No. 357. *Counterfeit, Durango,* 1829. (b.)
Weight, gr 1.000. Fineness, 707—1000ths. Hort. Value, $0.778.
Compare with No. 157. Eagle's head defective.

No. 358. *Counterfeit, Durango,* 1829. (c.)
Weight, gr 0.980. Fineness, near 700—1000ths. Value, $0.762.
Compare with No. 157. Eagle's beak defective.

No. 359. *Counterfeit, Durango,* 1829. (d.)
Weight, gr 1.000. Fineness, near 650—1000ths. Value, $0.722.
Compare with No. 157. Snake's neck too long.

No. 360. ***Counterfeit, Durango,*** **1830.** (a.)

Weight, $"0.870. Fineness, 572—1000ths. Hort. Value, $0.553.

Compare with No. 157. Snake's head too high.

No. 361. ***Counterfeit, Durango,*** **1830.** (b.)

Weight, $"0.990. Fineness near 750—1000ths. Value, $0.825.

Compare with No. 157. Letters defective or imperfect.

No. 362. ***Counterfeit, Durango,*** **1830 .** (c.)

Weight, $"0.960. Fineness, near 720—1000ths. Value, $0.768.

Compare with No. 157. Left wing too high.

No. 363. ***Counterfeit, Durango,* 1831.** (a.)
Weight, $ʷ0.820. Fineness, 683—1000ths. Hort. Value, $0.622.
Compare with No. 157. Snake's neck too near eagle's head.

No. 364. ***Counterfeit, Durango,* 1831.** (b.)
Weight, $ʷ0.900. Fineness, near 150—1000ths. Value, $0.150.
Compare with No. 157. Snake's head and neck too large, body too small.

No. 365. ***Counterfeit, or debased Durango,* 1832.** (a.)
Weight, $ʷ0.950. Fineness, 310—1000ths. Hort. Value, $0.327.
Stamp perfect, or nearly so. Compare with No. 159. Projection from the back of the eagle's head wanting. Very common.

No. 366. ***Counterfeit, Durango,* 1832.** (b.)
Weight, $"0.890. Fineness, near 3—1000ths. Value, **$0.030.**
Compare with No. 158. **Snake's head too small, eagle's plumage too fine.**

No. 367. ***Counterfeit, Durango,* 1833.** (a.)
Weight, $"0.980. Fineness, near 240—1000ths. Value, **$0.261.**
Compare with No. 159. Eagle's neck too straight.

No. 368. ***Counterfeit, Durango,* 1833.** (b.)
Weight, $"0.930. Fineness, 374—1000ths. Hort. **Value, $0.386**
Compare with No. 159. Eagle's neck too long.

No. 369. ***Counterfeit, Durango,* 1833.** (c.)

Weight, $"0.890. Fineness, 262—1000ths. Hort. Value, $0.259.

Compare with No. 159. Eagle's head too high.

No. 370. ***Counterfeit, Durango,* 1834.** (a.)

Weight, $"0.920. Fineness, 360—1000ths. Hort. Value, **$0.368.**

Compare with No. 159. Snake's neck and head rather too large. A good imitation.

No. 371. ***Counterfeit, Durango,* 1834.** (b.)

Weight, $"0.900. Fineness, 282—1000ths. Hort. Value, **$0.282.**

Stamp like 1832, (a.), No. 365, nearly perfect. Compare with No. 159. Head of the eagle not crested. Very common.

18

No. 372. ***Counterfeit, Durango,* 1834.** (c.)

Weight, $\$$'0.880. Fineness, 251—1000ths. Hort. Value, $\$$0.245.

Compare with No. 159. Rays too nearly even in length.

No. 373. ***Debased or Counterfeit, Durango,* 1836.**

Weight, $\$$'0.920. Fineness, 377—1000ths. Hort. Value, $\$$0.385.

Stamp like 1834, (b.) No. 371, nearly perfect. Compare with Nos. 159, 160. Eagle's head not crested.

No. 374. ***Debased Dollar or Counterfeit, Durango,* 1837.**

Weight, $\$$'0.960. Fineness, 744—1000ths. Hort. Value, $\$$0.793.

Compare with No. 160. Nearly if not quite identical. Crest of the eagle too large.

No. 375. ***Counterfeit, Durango,*** **1838.**

Weight, $"0.940. Fineness, 575—1000ths. Hort. Value, $0.605.

Compare with No. 160. Eagle s neck too straight.

No. 376. ***Counterfeit, Durango,*** **1839.** (a.)

Weight, $"1.000. Fineness, 450—1000ths. Hort. Value, $0.500.

A large number of these dollars in general circulation. Compare with No. 161, D. wrong side up after 10. Rays wrong.

No. 377. ***Counterfeit, Durango,*** **1839.** (b.)

Weight, $"0.960. Fineness, 514—1000ths. Hort. Value, $0.548.

Compare with No. 161. Rays oblique

No. 378. ***Counterfeit, Durango,*** **1839.** (c.)
Weight, $"1.060. Fineness, near 5—1000ths. Value, $0.060.
Compare with No. 161. Eagle's neck too straight.

No. 379. ***Debased Dollar, Durango,*** **1839,** (d.)
Weight, $"0.980. Fineness, 750—1000ths. H o r t. Value, $0.816.
Compare with Nos. 160, 161. Stamp nearly or quite identical with No. 160.

No. 380. ***Counterfeit, Durango,*** **1840.** (a.)
Weight, $"1.000. Fineness, near 300—1000ths. Value, $0.333.
Compare with No. 161. Eagle's head too low.

No. 381. *Debased Dollar or Counterfeit, Durango,* 1840. (b.)

Weight, $w 0.930. Fineness, 650—1000ths. Hort. Value, $0.671.

Compare with Nos. 160, 161. King die portions (cap and rays, eagle, &c.,) apparently same as No. 160. Lettering irregular.

No. 382. *Counterfeit, Durango,* date effaced.

Weight, $w 0.980. Fineness, near 450—1000ths. Value, $0.490.

COUNTERFEIT MEXICAN DOLLARS.

Mint of San Luis Potosi. Mint Mark, Pi

No. 383. *Counterfeit, Potosi,* 1826.

Weight, $w 0.850. Fineness, near 270—1000ths. Value, $0.255.

No. 384. ***Counterfeit, Potosi,* 1827.**

Weight, $"0.820. Fineness, 150—1000ths. H o r t. Value, $0.136.

Compare with No. 163. Eagle's beak too blunt.

No. 385. ***Counterfeit, Potosi,* 1829.**

Weight, $"1.000. Fineness, 280—1000ths. H o r t. Value, $0.311.

Compare with No. 164. Vines different. Eagle's head too near the snake's head.

No. 386. ***Counterfeit, Potosi,* 1830.**

Weight, $"1.030. Fineness, 335—1000ths. H o r t. Value, $0.383.

Compare with No. 164. Vines widely different.

No. 387. ***Counterfeit, Potosi,* 1832.**

Weight, $"0.820. Fineness, 216—1000ths. Hort. Value, $0.196.

Compare with No. 164. Lettering too small.

No. 388. ***Counterfeit, Potosi,* 1834.**

Weight, $"0.850. Fineness, 285—1000ths. Hort. Value, $0.269.

An excellent imitation, yet not from the same dies as No. 166, which see. Left wing too short.

No. 389. ***Counterfeit, Potosi,* 1835.** (a.)

Weight, $"0.90. Fineness, 337—1000ths. Hort. Value, $0.337.

Compare with No. 167. Snake's head too far from eagle's head.

No. 390. ***Counterfeit, Potosi,*** **1835.** (b.)

Weight, $"1.000. Fineness, 210—1000ths. H o r t. Value, **$0.233.**

Very common. Compare with No. 167. **Letters MEX irregular.**

No. 391. ***Counterfeit, Potosi,*** **1836.** (a.)

Weight, $"0.810. Fineness, near 200—1000ths. **Value, $0.180.**

Compare with No. 167. **Snake's head too far from eagle's head.**

No. 392. ***Counterfeit, Potosi,*** **1836.** (b.)

Weight, $"0.960. Fineness, 120—1000ths. H o r t. **Value $0.123**

Compare with No. 167. **Snake's neck too short.**

No. 393. ***Counterfeit, Potosi,* 1843.** (a.)
Weight, ^{ozs}0.950. Fineness, near **150—1000ths**. Value, **$0.158.**
Compare with No. 169. Rays and plumage defective.

No. 394. ***Counterfeit, Potosi,* 1843.** (b.)
Weight, ^{ozs}1.000. Fineness, near **450—100ths**. Value, **$0.500.**
Compare with No. 169. Eagle's wings too broad near the body.

No. 395. ***Counterfeit, Potosi,* 1844.**
Weight, ^{ozs}0.900. Fineness, near **460—1000ths**. Value, **$0.460.**
19 Compare with No. 170. Snake's neck too long.

DEBASED AND COUNTERFEIT MEXICAN DOLLARS.
Mint of Guadalaxara. Mint Mark, G^a.

No. 396. ***Counterfeit, Guadalaxara,*** **1827.**
Weight, $"0.820. Fineness, near 13—1000ths. Value, $0.010.
Compare with No. 180. Snake's neck bent too much down.

No. 397. ***Counterfeit, Guadalaxara,*** **1831.**
Weight, $"1.050. Fineness, 550—1000ths. Hort. Value, $0.641.
Compare with No. 180. Snake's body too small and straight.

No. 398. ***Debased Dollar, Guadalaxara,*** **1838.**
Weight, $0"8.30. Fineness, near 630—1000ths. Value, $0.581.
Compare with No. 180. The stamp is genuine. This coin probably issued from the mint.

No. 399. ***Counterfeit, Guadalaxara,*** **1841.**

Weight, $"0.730. Fineness, 15—1000ths. Hort. Value, $0.012.

Copper coated with silver. Compare with Nos. 181, 182. Wings too broad near the body. Right vine different.

No. 400. ***Counterfeit, Guadalaxara,*** **1842.**

Weight, $"0.970. Fineness, near 360—1000ths. Value, $0.388.

Compare with No. 181. Snake's body too small.

COUNTERFEIT MEXICAN DOLLARS.

Mint Marks obscure, anomalous or irregular, viz: E° M°—M^s—G.—D°—D.—°D.—P.—T. F.—P°

No. 401. ***Counterfeit,*** **Mint Mark Obscure, 1826.**

Weight, $"0.160. Fineness, near 180—1000ths. Value, $0.212.

No. 402. ***Counterfeit***, E°M° **1828.**

Weight, $"1.020. Fineness, near 720—1000ths. Value, $0.816.

Compare with No. 132. Snake's head bent down too much.

No. 403 ***Counterfeit***, Ms **1838.** (a.)

Weight, $"0.880. Fineness, 438—1000ths. H o r t. Value, $0.428.

No. 404. ***Counterfeit***, Ms **1838.** (b.)

Weight, $"0.850. Fineness, near 320—1000ths. Value, $0.302.

No. 405. ***Counterfeit***, M^s **1840.**
Weight, $"0.900. Fineness, near 85—1000ths. Value, $0.085.

No. 406. ***Counterfeit***, G. **1827.**
Weight, $"0.830. Fineness, near 5—1000ths. Value, $0.004.

No. 407. ***Counterfeit***, G. **1830.**
Weight, $"0.970. Fineness, near 18—1000ths. Value, $0.019.
Plated.

No. 408. ***Counterfeit,*** **G. 1831.**
Weight, $"0.960. Fineness, near 360—1000ths. Value, **$0.384.**

No. 409. ***Counterfeit,*** **G. 1832.**
Weight, $"1.020. Fineness, near 180—1000ths. Value, **$0.204.**

No. 410. ***Counterfeit,*** **G. 1837.**
Weight, $"0.810. Fineness, 529—1000ths. H o r t. **Value, $0.476.**

No. 411. ***Counterfeit,*** G. **1838.**

Weight, $"0.910. Fineness, near 510—1000ths. Value $0.515.

No. 412. ***Counterfeit,*** G. **1840.**

Weight, $"1.030. Fineness, near 90—1000ths. Value $0.103.

No. 413. ***Counterfeit,*** G. **1842.**

Weight, $"0.960. Fineness, near 5—1000ths. Value, $0.005.

No. 414. ***Counterfeit*****, D^s^ 1826.**

Weight, ^{gr}1.000. Fineness, 258—1000ths. H o r t. Value, $0.286.

No. 415. ***Counterfeit*****, D^s^ 1832.**

Weight, ^{gr}1.000. Fineness, 255—1000ths. H o r t. **Value, $0.283.**

Date 1839, same stamp observed.

No. 416. ***Counterfeit*****, D^s^ 1835.**

Weight, ^{gr}0.940. Fineness, near 81—1000ths. Value, $0.084.

No. 417. ***Counterfeit***, **D.[s] 1836.**

Weight, $′′0.920. Fineness, near 210—1000ths. Value, $0.214.

No. 418. ***Counterfeit***, **D. 1833.**

Weight, $′′0.840. Fineness, 0—1000ths. Value, $0.000.

No. 419. ***Counterfeit***, **°D. 1830.**

Weight, $′′0.920. Fineness, near 5—1000ths. Value, $0.005.

20

No. 420. ***Counterfeit,*** °D. **1840.**
Weight, $"0.860. Fineness, 25—1000ths. Hort. Value, **$0.023.**

No. 421. ***Counterfeit,*** P. **1829.**
Weight, $"0.840. Fineness, 415—1000ths. Hort. Value, $0.387.

No. 422. ***Counterfeit,*** P. **1832.**
Weight, $"1.070. Fineness, near 540—1000ths. Value, $0.642.

No. 423. ***Counterfeit*, P. 1839.**

Weight, $''0.810. Fineness, 450—1000ths. Hort. Value, $0.405.

No. 424. ***Counterfeit*, T. F. 1835.**

Weight, $''0.960. Fineness, near 300—1000ths. Value, $0.320.

No. 425. ***Counterfeit*, I^{s} 1840.**

Weight, $''1.000. Fineness, near 450—1000ths. Value, $0.500.

REMARKS UPON DEBASED MEXICAN DOLLARS, BEARING IMPRESSIONS APPARENTLY GENUINE.

After a careful inspection and comparison of Nos. 365, 370, 371, 373, 374, 379, 381 of the Durango Dollars; and Nos. 324, 334, 335, 345 of the Guanaxuato Dollars, I am iuduced to entertain the following opinion:— That at least one pair of dies, (king dies perhaps,) corresponding essentially to No. 146, has been probably removed from the Mint of Guanaxuato, and made subservient to the production of a base coinage, represented by the Nos. 324, &c., above quoted; and that there has probably been a similar removal and prostitution of one or two pairs of dies from the Mint of Durango, said dies essentially corresponding to No. 159 of this work. It can hardly be supposed that base and fraudulent money would be manufactured systematically in those mints, the great majority of whose Dollars stand so deservedly fair; and since, therefore, the impressions alluded to, appear genuine, it seems probable that the dies were abstracted.

I here subjoin, as relevant to the subject, a note addressed to the Assayer of the New Orleans Mint, with his reply.

BRANCH MINT, NEW ORLEANS,
June 16th, 1845.

DR. WM. P. HORT, *Assayer*:

SIR,—You will oblige me by communicating to me the substance of certain information which you possess, relative to the existence of debased or depreciated Mexican Dollars, bearing the genuine stamps, to which matter I am aware your attention was called a few years since,

And oblige, yours truly,

J. L. RIDDELL.

BRANCH MINT, NEW ORLEANS,
16th June, 1845.

SIR,—I have read your note of this day's date. I have much pleasure in imparting whatever information I possess relative to the subject matter of your enquiry.

In 1838, at the commencement of the operations of this Mint, the average title of Mexican Dollars was supposed to be 897.* The result of our experience, however, did not correspond with that average. Deposits of Mexican Dollars averaged at different tmes, from 1838 to 1841, 860,† 880, 890, 894, 897, 900. A little attention to the subject explained the cause. More or less counterfeits were found in almost every deposit; and some were so admirably well executed as to render their detection impossible without an assay. These I considered as debased or depreciated coins, not properly counterfeit. They were, at the time referred to, very abundant in this city. My opinion was confirmed by a gentleman who had resided many years in Mexico, who informed me that the old dies could be purchased at certain Mints, remote from the Capital; that they were sent to Europe, where new dies (fac-smilies) were manufactured, and that with the dies so procured, Dollars were stamped, and an immense number thrown

* 897—100ths fine. † 860—1000ths, &c.

into circulation. There is reason to believe that this information was correct, for a communication on the subject, which I had inserted in one of our daily papers, attracted the attention of the Mexican Consul here, who apprized his Government of it. Shortly after, a proclamation on the subject issued from the Government of Mexico, and since that time the particular Dollars of which I have been speaking, have become comparatively rare.

Truly yours,

WM. P. HORT, *Assayer*.

DR. J. L. RIDDELL,
Melter & Refiner, *Br. Mint*, *N. O.*

These debased Dollars can usually be distinguished by rubbing them smartly on a soft board, until a bright and new metalic surface is attained; then rub the fingers over the surface, after which, by reflected daylight, the pale brassy or coppery hue of the debased silver may be discerned. The hints which I have given under each, in its proper place, will also be found useful, and oftentimes sufficient. It should be borne in mind that they are always wanting in specific gravity or density; and though irregular in weight, they are most frequently too light.

For convenient reference, in connection with this subject, the fac-simile figures, Nos. 146 and 159, are here again inserted. In explanation of the way in which the Mexican working dies of various dates, are probably got up from the same original dies or parts of dies, the reader is referred to the remarks on Mexican Dollars, preceding No. 121.

No. 146.

No. 159.

AMERICAN HALF DOLLARS, OR HALF DOLLARS OF THE UNITED STATES.

Nos. 426 to 439 inclusive.

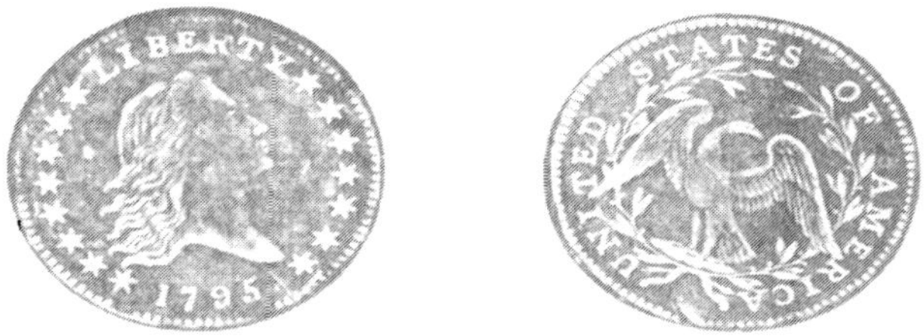

No. 426. ***American Half Dollar*, 1795.**

Stamp of 1794, 1795.

Weight, $0.504=208 grs.=13.476 grms.
Fineness, 892—1000ths. Value, $0.499½=2*s.* 0.7*d.*=2.67 fr.

No. 427. ***American Half Dollar*, 1806.**

Stamp of 1806, 1807.

Weight, $0.504=208 grs.=13.476 grms.
Fineness, 892—1000ths. Value, $0.499½=2*s.* 0.7*d.*=2.67 fr.

No. 428. ***American Half Dollar*, 1808.**

Weight, $0.504=208 grs.=13.476 grms.
Fineness, 892—1000ths. Value, $0.499½=2*s.* 0.7*d.*=2.67 fr.

No. 429. ***American Half Dollar*, 1817.**

Stamp of 1809 to 1818 inclusive.

Weight, $"0.504.=208 grs.=13.476 grms.
Fineness, 892—1000ths. Value, $0.499½=2*s*. 0.7*d*.=2.67 fr.

For Counterfeits, vide Nos. 440, 441, 442.

No. 430. ***American Half Dollar*, 1830.**

Stamp of 1819 to 1833 inclusive.

Weight, $"1.504=208 grs.=13.476 grms.
Fineness, 892—1000ths. Value, $0.499½=2*s*. 0.7*d*.=2.67 fr.

For Counterfeits, vide Nos. 433 to 466.

No. 431. ***American Half Dollar*, 1836.**

Stamp of 1834, 1835, 1836.

Weight, $"0.504=208 grs.=13.476 grms.
Fineness, 892½—1000ths. Value, $0.500.=2*s*. 0.7*d*=2. 67 fr.

For Counterfeits, vide Nos. 467, 468, 469, 470.

No. 432. *American Half Dollar*, 1836.

Weight, $"0.504=208 grs.=13.476 grms
Fineness, 893—1000ths.
Value, $0.500=2*s.* 0.7*d.*=2.67 fr.

Vide Counterfeit, No. 471:

No 433. *American Half Dollar*, 1837.

Weight, $"0.500=206.25 grs.=13.363 grms.
Fineness, 900—1000ths.
Value, $0.500=2*s.* 0.7*d.*=2.67 fr.

Vide Counterfeit, No. 472.

No. 434. *American Half Dollar*, 1838. (a.)

Pattern stamp. Few ever left the mint, if any.
Cabinet of the Mint, Philadelphia.

No. 435. ***American Half Dollar*, 1838.** (b.)

Pattern Stamp.

Cabinet of the Mint, Philadelphia.

No. 336. ***American Half Dollar*, 1838.** (c.)

Pattern Stamp.

Cabinet of the Mint, Philadelphia.

No. 437. ***American Half Dollar*, 1839.**

Stamp of 1338, 1839.

Weight, $"0.500=206.25 grs.=13.363 grms.
Fineness, 900—1000ths.
Value, $0.500=2*s.* 0.7*d.* =2.67 fr.

21 For Counterfeits, see Nos. 473, to 477 inclusive.

No. 438. ***American Half Dollar*, 1840.**

Stamp of 1839, 1840, 1841.

Weight, $"0.500=206.25 grs.=13.363 grms.
Fineness, 900—1000ths.
Value, $0.500=2s. 0.7*d.*=2.67 fr.

No. 439. ***American Half Dollar*, 1843.**

Stamp of 1842, 1843, 1844, 1845.

Weight, $"0.500=206.25 grs.=13.363 grms.
Fineness, 900—1000ths. Value, $0.500=2*s.* 0.7*d.*=2.67 fr.

Mint at New Orleans, designated by O.

COUNTERFEIT AMERICAN HALF DOLLARS.

No. 440. ***Counterfeit Half Dollar*, 1814.**

Weight, $"0.480. Fineness, near 150—100ths. Value, $0.080.

Compare with No. 430. Rays of the stars too short, upper arrow shaft too long, letters imperfect.

No. 441. *Counterfeit Half Dollar*, 1817.

Weight, $"0.440. Fineness, near 270—1000ths. Value, $0.132.

Compare with No. 429. The E in STATES too low. F in OF too low. In the genuine coin the greatest measurement across the bust is near 1 inch and $\frac{3}{32}$ of an inch, while in this it is near $\frac{1}{20}$ of an inch less. A good imitation.

No. 442. *Counterfeit Half Dollar*, 1818.

Weight, $"0.410. Fineness, near 180—1000ths. Value, $0.082.

Compare with No. 429. Eagle's head too large. 50 C. defective.

No. 443. *Counterfeit Half Dollar*, 1821.

Weight, $"0.440. Fineness, 357—1000ths. Hort. Value, $0.173.

Compare with No. 430. Greatest measurement of the bust 0.07=7—100ths of an inch too short, figures of the date defective.

No. 444. ***Counterfeit Half Dollar*, 1822.**

Weight, $"0.480. Fineness, near 180—1000ths. Value, $0.096.

Compare with No. 430. Feathering upon the arrow shafts too finely wrought; eagle's beak too near the right wing.

No. 445. ***Counterfeit Half Dollar*, 1823.**

Weight, $"0.500. Fineness, 406—1000ths. H o r t. Value, $0.225.

Compare with No. 430. Eagle's beak too near the right wing

No. 446. ***Counterfeit Half Dollar*, 1824.**

Weight, $"0.370. Fineness, 265—1000ths. H o r t.
Value, $0.108.

Compare with No. 430. The E in UNITED, and STATES, too broad. The Ts and F, also defective. Eagle's mouth too much open.

No. 447. ***Counterfeit Half Dollar*, 1825.**

Weight, $\text{\$}$"0.440. Fineness, 237—1000ths. Hort. Value, $0.115.

Compare with No. 430. Figures rather clumsy, feathering upon the arrow shafts too finely wrought.

No. 448. ***Counterfeit Half Dollar*, 1826.** (a.)

Weight, $"0.480. Fineness, near 180—1000ths. Value, $0.096.

Compare with No. 430. 5 in 50 too small, eagles's beak too near his right wing.

No. 449. ***Counterfeit Half Dollar*, 1826.** (b.)

Weight, $"0.550. Fineness, 200—1000ths. Hort. Value, $0.122.

Compare with No. 430. Figures of the date too large, rays of the stars too slender, lettering defective

No. 450. ***Counterfeit Half Dollar*, 1827.**

Weight, $"0.410. Fineness, 237—1000ths. Value, $0.108.

Compare with No. 430. Greatest measurement across the bust too short, 8 rather too large, relation of the neighboring shafts and heads of arrows defective.

No. 451. ***Counterfeit Half Dollar*, 1828.** (a.)

Weight, $"0.500. Fineness, near 90—1000ths. Value, $0.050.

Compare with No. 430. Rays of the stars too slim, E in UNITED defective, upper arrow head too long.

No. 452. ***Counterfeit Half Dollar*, 1828.** (b.)

Weight, $"0.400. Fineness, near 300—1000ths. Value, $0.133.

Compare with No. 430. Greatest measurement of bust too short, C after 50 too large. Admirably executed.

No. 453. ***Counterfeit Half Dollar*, 1828.** (c.)
Weight, $"0.470. Fineness, near 360—1000ths. Value, $0.188.
Compare with No. 430. Lettering defective, stars and bust wrongly made.

No. 454. ***Counterfeit Half Dollar*, 1829.** (a.)
Weight, $"0.520. Fineness, 195—1000ths. H o r't. Value, $0.112.
Compare with No. 430. Figures and letters badly made. Hair on the bust downy.

No. 455. ***Counterfeit Half Dollar*, 1829.** (b.)
Weight, $"0.380. Fineness, 334—1000ths. H o r t.
Value, $0.141.
Compare with No. 430. Letters too small

No. 456. *Counterfeit Half Dollar*, 1830.
Weight, $"0.500. Fineness, near 360—1000ths. Value, **$0.200.**
Compare with No. 430. Eagle's beak too near the right wing.

No. 457. *Counterfeit Half Dollar*, 1831.
Weight, $"0.410. Fineness, near 90—1000ths. Value, **$0.041**
Compare with No. 430. Letters too small.

No. 458. *Counterfeit Half Dollar*, 1832. (a.)
Weight, $"0.500. Fineness, near 267—1000ths. Value, **$0.148.**
Compare with No. 430. Letters too small and irregular, eagle's beak too slender.

No. 459. ***Counterfeit Half Dollar*, 1832.** (b.)

Weight, $"0.380. Fineness, near 270—1000ths. Value, $0.114.

Compare with No. 430. Eagle's beak too near the right wing.

No. 460. ***Counterfeit Half Dollar*, 1832.** (c.)

Weight, $"0.450. Fineness, near 360—1000ths. Value, $0.180.

Compare with No. 430. Eagle's beak too near the right wing.

No. 461. ***Counterfeit Half Dollar*, 1833.** (a.)

Weight, $"0.520. Fineness, near 360—1000ths. Value, $0.208.

Compare with No. 430. Shafts of the arrows too long. Letters badly made.

22

No. 462. *Counterfeit Half Dollar*, 1833. (b.)
Weight, $"0.430. Fineness, near 450—1000ths. Value, **$0.215.**
Compare with No. 430. **Bust too small, 50 C. too small.**

No. 463. *Counterfeit Half Dollar*, 1833. (c.)
Weight, $"0.530. Fineness, 267—1000ths. H o r t. **Value, $0.157.**
Compare with No. 430. Eagle's head too small, **letters small and irregular.**

No. 464. *Counterfeit Half Dollar*, 1833. (d.)
Weight, $"0.420. Fineness and Value, 0. H o r t.
German silver. Compare with No. 430. **Stars too small, letters bad.**

No. 465. ***Counterfeit Half Dollar*, 1833.** (e.)

Weight, $"0.430. Fineness, 368—1000ths. H o r t. Value, $0.175.

Compare with No. 430. Greatest measurement across the bust too short. Lower stars at the back of the bust too small.

No. 466. ***Counterfeit Half Dollar*, 1833.** (f.)

Weight, $"0.460. Fineness, near 300—1000ths. Value, $0.153.

Compare with No. 430. Profile of the bust wrong, arrow heads too small.

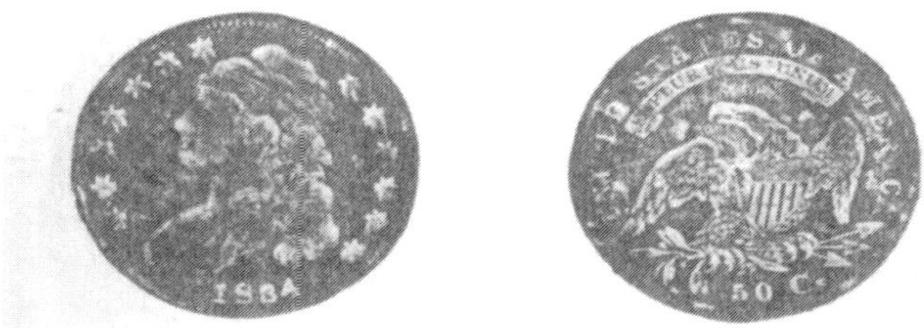

No. 467. ***Counterfeit Half Dollar*, 1834.** (a.)

Weight, $"0.430. Fineness, 354—1000ths. H o r t.

Value. $0.168.

Compare with No. 431. Stars too large.

No. 468. ***Counterfeit Half Dollar*, 1834.** (b.)
Weight, 8"0.410. Fineness, and Value, 0. Hort.

A kind of German silver. Compare with No. 431. **Stars too large, figures of the date too large.**

No. 469. ***Counterfeit Half Dollar*, 1836.** (a.)
Weight, 8"0.450. Fineness, 295—1000ths. Hort.
Value, $0.147.

Compare with No. 431. Profile wrong, **letters bad, arrow heads too small.**

No. 470. ***Counterfeit Half Dollar*, 1836.** (b.)
Weight, 8"0.450. Fineness, 295—1000ths. Hort.
Value, $0.147.

Compare with No. 431. **Letters and figures bad.**

No. 471. ***Counterfeit Half Dollar*, O. 1836.** (c.)
Weight, $"0.410. Fineness, near 1—1000ths. Value, $0.000½.

A base alloy galvanised. Compare with No. 432. Letters irregular. Eagle's head too large. HALF DOL. instead of 50 CENTS.

No. 472. ***Counterfeit Half Dollar*, 1837.**
Weight, $"0.460. Fineness, and Value 0.

German silver. Compare with No. 433. Profile wrong, letters bad.

No. 473. ***Counterfeit Half Dollar*, 1838.** (a.)
Weight, $"0.430. Fineness, 0—1000ths. Value, $0.000.

Appears to be German silver. Compare with No. 437. Stars and figures of the date defective, leaves of the olive branch rather too small.

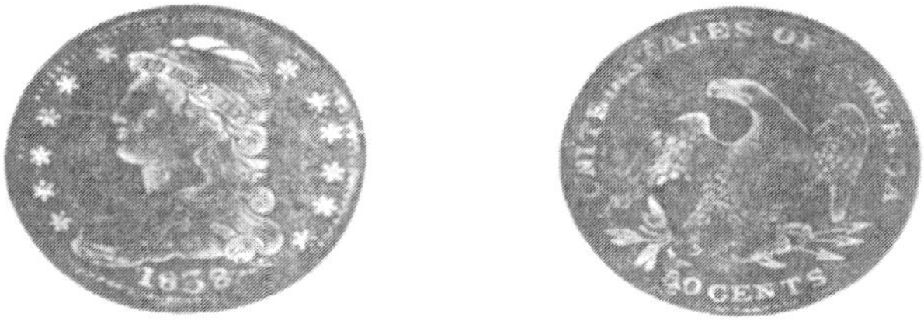

No. 474. *Counterfeit Half Dollar*, 1838. (b.)

Weight, $"0.420. Fineness, 0—1000ths. Value, $0.000.

Brassy German silver, very thinly silver-washed. Compare with No. 437. Stars too large, letters too small.

No. 475. *Counterfeit Half Dollar*, O. 1839. (a.)

Weight, $"0.480. Fineness, near 1—1000ths. Value, $0.000½.

A base alloy galvanized over with silver. Compare with No. 437. Letters irregular. The O, under the bust, is the mint-mark of the New Orleans Branch Mint.

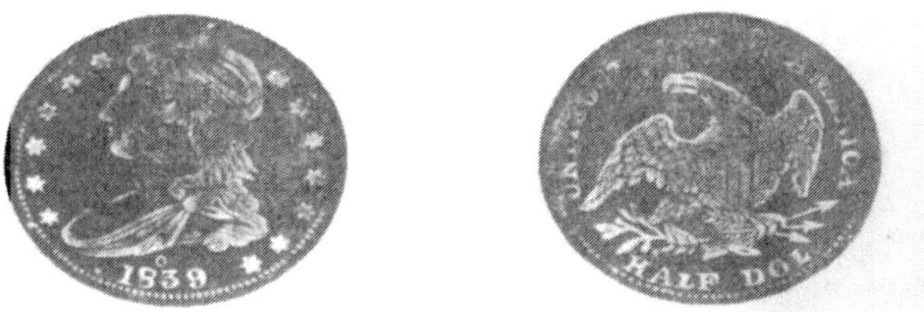

No. 476. *Counterfeit Half Dollar*, O. 1839. (b.)

Weight, $"0.480. Fineness, near 1—1000ths. Value, $0.000½.

An alloy of copper, tin, &c. galvanized. Compare with No. 437. Letters irregular.

No. 477. *Counterfeit Half Dollar*, O. 1839. (c.)
Weight, $"0.490. Fineness, near 1—1000ths. Value, $0.000¼.

Seems to be an alloy like type metal with copper, and to have been cast, as the impression is not as distinct as in the genuine coin. Dies genuine. Compare with No. 437.

FRANCO-AMERICAN HALF CROWN, OR HALF DOLLAR.

This curious coin, in my possession, is the only one of the kind existing so far as I know.

Obverse, a turretted and laureated bust of what is intended, probably, as the Goddess of Liberty. Legend, FRANCO AMERICANA COLONIA, the *French American Colonies.* CASTORLAND, and the date in the exergue.

Reverse, apparently Ceres holding in her right hand a horn of plenty; in her left a carpenter's brace and bit, with a sugar maple tree, from which sap is flowing into a tub. At the feet of Ceres is a sheaf of grain. Legend, SALVE MAGNA PARENS FRUGUM, *Save or regard us, great parent of fruits.* A beaver is in the exergue. The milling on the edge is indented like modern English and American coins.

No. 478. *Franco-American Silver Coin*, 1796.
Weight, $"0.500=206.25 grs.=13.363 grms.
Fineness, apparently near 900—1000ths.
Value, $0.500=2*s.* 0.7*d.*=2.67 fr.

HALF DOLLAR OF SIERRA LEONE.

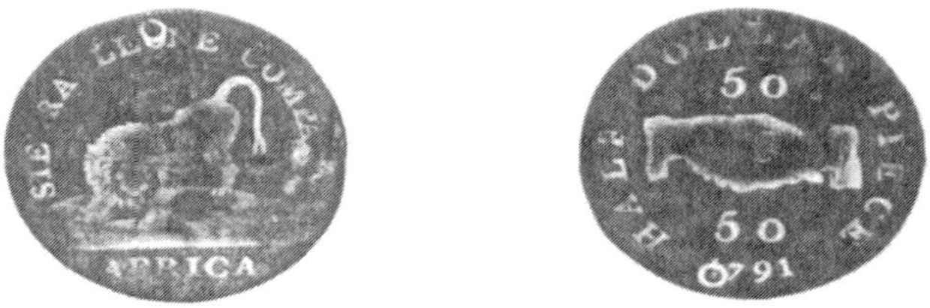

No. 479. ***Half Dollar of the Sierra Leone Company, Africa,* 1791.**

Weight, $″0.495=204.18 grs.=13.22 grms.
Fineness, 816—1000ths. B o n n e v i l l e.
Value, $0.450=1*s.* 10.2*d.*=2.41 fr.

SPANISH HALF DOLLARS.

Nos. 480 to 498 inclusive.

No. 480. ***Spanish Half Dollar?* 1684.**

Weight, $″0.450=185.62 grs.=12.026 grms.
Fineness, probably near 906—1000ths.
Value, $0.453=1*s.* 10.4*d.*=2.43 fr.

No. 481. ***Spanish Half Dollar.* 1776:**

With Chinese markings.

Weight, $″0.490=202.12 grs.=13.09 grms.
Fineness, 900—1000ths. Value, $0.490=2*s.* 0.1*d.*=2.62 fr.

This piece having been worn, is light.

No. 482. ***Spanish Half Dollar*, 1777.**

Weight, $"0.495=204.18 grs.=13.22 grms.
Fineness, 900—1000ths.
Value, $0.495=2*s*. 0.4*d*.=2.65 fr.

No. 483. ***Spanish Half Dollar*, 1810.**

Weight, $"0.500=206 25 grs.=13.363 grms.
Fineness, 900—1000ths.
Value, $0.500=2*s*. 0.7*d*.=2.67 fr.

No. 484. ***Spanish Half Dollar*, 1816.**

Weight, $"0.500=206.25 grs.=13.363 grms.
Fineness, 900—1000ths.
Value, $0.500=2*s*. 0.7*d*.=2.67 fr.

23

No. 485. *Spanish Half Dollar*, 1821.
Weight, $"0.504=208 grs.=13.47 grms.
Fineness, 920—1000ths. E c k f e l d t & D u b o i s.
Value, $0.515=2*s.* 1.4*d.*=2. 75 fr.

No. 486. *Spanish American Half Dollar*, 1767.
Mint of Potosi, S. A.
Weight, $"0.500=206.25 grs.=13.363 grms.
Fineness, 906—1000ths. B o n n e v i l l e.
Value, $0.503=2*s.* 0.8*d.*=2.68 fr.

No. 487. *Spanish American Half Dollar Medal.* 1796.
Weight, $"0.510=210.37 grs.=13.63 grms.
Fineness, near 900—1000ths. Value, $0.510=2*s.* 1.2*d.*=2.73 fr.

No. 488. ***Spanish American Cob Half Dollar, or Mexican Half Dollar,*** **1811.**

Weight, $w0.495=204 grs.=13.23 grms.
Fineness, near 900—1000ths. Value, $0.495=2*s.* 0.3*d.*=2.64 fr.

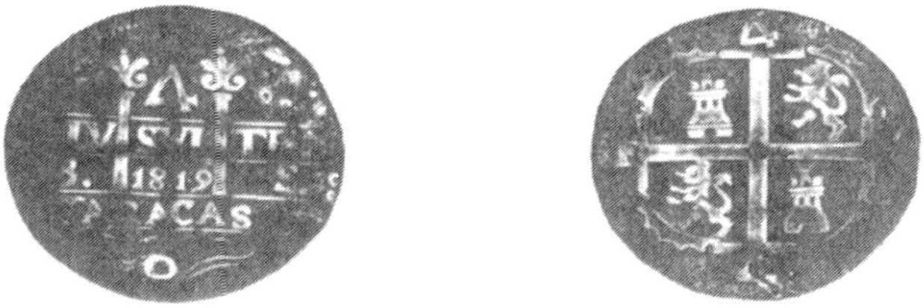

No. 489. ***Spanish American Half Dollar, Carracas,*** **1819.**

Weight, $w0.420=173.25 grs.=11.22 grms
Fineness, apparently near 900—1000ths,
Value, $0.420.=1*s.* 8.7*d.*=2.24 fr.

This piece of 4 reals seems much finer than those of two reals. The latter are reported by Eckfeldt & Dubois to be 690—1000ths fine.

No. 490. ***Spanish American Half Dollar,*** **1780.**

Mint of Mexico

Weight, $w0.495=204 grs.=13.23 grms.
Fineness, 900—1000ths. Eckfeldt & Dubois
Value, $0.495=2*s.* 0.3*d.*=2.64 fr.

No. 491. ***Spanish American Half Dollar.***

Mint of Mexico, 1807.

Weight, **$"0.500=206.25 grs.=13.363 grms**
Fineness, **898—1000ths.** Value, **$0.498=2*s.* 0.6*d.*=2.66 fr.**

No. 492. ***Spanish American Half Dollar.***

Mint of Santiago, 1807.

Weight, **$"0.495=204 grs.=13.22 grms.**
Fineness, 898—1000ths. Value, **$0.493=2*s.* 0.3*d.*=2.63 fr.**

No. 493. ***Spanish American Half Dollar.***

Mint of New Guatemala, 1807.

Weight, **$"0.500=206.25 grs.=13.363 grms.**
Fineness, **897—1000ths.** Value, **$0.498=2*s.* 0.4*d.*=2.65 fr.**

No. 494. *Spanish American Half Dollar*, 1808.
Mint of Potosi, S. A.
Weight, $"0.495=204 grs.=13.23 grms.
Fineness, 898—1000ths. Value, $0.494=2*s.* 0.3*d.*=2.64 fr.

No. 495. *Spanish American Half Dollar*,
Mint of Lima, Peru, 1811.
Weight, $"0.485=200 grs.=12.95 grms.
Fineness, 900—1000ths. Value, $0.485=1*s.* 11.9*d.*=2.59 fr.

No. 496. *Hispano-Mexican Half Dollar*.
Mint of Guadalaxara, 1814.
Weight, $"0.500=206.25 grs.=13.363 grms.
Fineness, probably near 880—1000ths. Value, $0.488=2*s.*=2.61 fr.

No. 497. ***Spanish American Half Dollar.***

Mint of New Guatemala, 1815.

Weight, $"0.500=206.25 grs.=13.363 grs.
Fineness, 896—1000ths. Value, $0.497=2*s.* 0.4*d.*=2.65 fr.

No. 498. ***Spanish American Half Dollar,***

Mint of Lima, Peru, 1817.

Weight, $"0.500=206.25 grs.=13.363 grms.
Fineness, 900—1000ths. Value, $0.500=2*s.* 0.7*d.*=2.67 fr.

SOUTH AMERICAN HALF DOLLARS.
Nos. 499 to 502.

No. 499. ***Half Dollar of La Plata,* 1813.**

Weight, $"0.500=206 25 grs.=13.363 grms.
Fineness, 888—1000ths. Eckelfeldt & Dubois.
Value, $0.493=2*s.* 0.2*d.*=2.63 fr.

No. 500. *Bolivian Half Dollar, Potosi,* 1830.
Weight, $"0.500=206.25 grs.=13.363 grms.
Fineness, 670—1000ths. Eckfeldt & Dubois.
Value, $0.371=1*s.* 6.2*d.*=1.98 fr.

No. 501. *Peruvian Half Dollar, Cuzco,* 1836.
Weight, $"0.500=206.25 grs.=13.363 grms.
Fineness, 650—1000ths.
Value, $0.361=1*s.* 5.7*d.*=1.92 fr.
This unusual debasement of the Peruvian Half Dollar was legalized from June, 1835, to February, 1838. Eckfeldt & Dubois, page 97.

No. 502. *Peruvian Half Dollar, Arequipa,* 1838.
Weight, $"0.500=206.25 grs.=13.363 grms.
Fineness, 660—1000ths. Eckfeldt & Dubois.
Value, $0.366=1*s.* 6*d.*=1.95 fr.

MEXICAN HALF DOLLARS.

Nos. 503 to 512, inclusive.

No. 503. ***Mexican Half Dollar, hammered.***

Vargas, Sombrerete. 1811.

Weight, $"470=193.87 grs.=12.56 grms.
Fineness, 885—1000ths. Value, $0.462=1*s.* 10.7*d.*=2.47 fr.

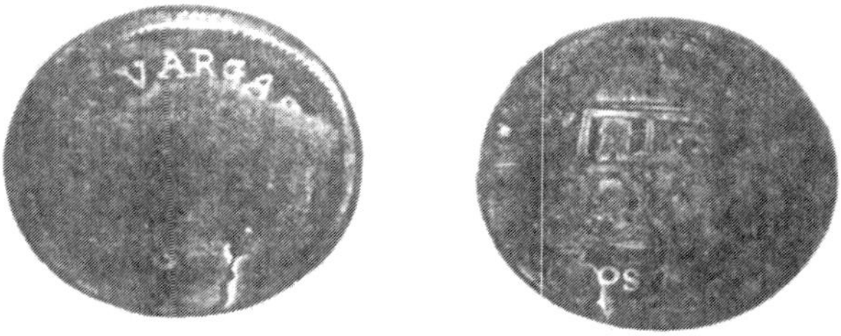

No. 504. ***Mexican Half Dollar, hammered.***

General Vargas. Sombrerete, 1811.

Weight, $"0.464=191.40 grs.=12.39 grms.
Fineness, 885—1000ths. Value, $0.456=1*s.* 10.5*d.*=2.44 fr.

No. 505. ***Mexican Half Dollar Medal.***

Weight, $"0.504=207.90 grs.=13.46 grms.
Fineness, 900—1000ths? Value, $0.504=2*s.* 0.9*d.*=2.69 fr.

No. 506. ***Mexican Half Dollar Medal.***
Weight, $^w0.530=218.62 grs.=14.16 grms.
Fineness, 900—1000ths ?
Value, $0.530=2*s.* 2.1*d.*=2.83 fr.

No. 507. ***Mexican Half Dollar, Zacatecas.***
Weight, $^w0.500=206.25 grs.=13.36 grms.
Fineness, 896—1000ths.
Value, $0.497=2*s.* 0.4*d.*=2.65 fr.

No. 508. ***Mexican Half Dollar, Zacatecas.***
Weight, $^w0.500=206.25 grs.=13.36 grms.
Fineness, 897—1000ths.
Value, $0.498=2*s.* 0.5*d.*=2.66 fr.

24

No. 509. ***Mexican Half Dollar, Zacatecas.***

Weight, $"0.500=206.25 grs.=13.36 grms.
Fineness, 898—1000ths. Value, $0.499=2*s.* 0.5*d.*=2.67 fr.

No. 510. ***Counterfeit Half Dollar, Zacatecas,*** **1837.**

Weight, $"0.440. Fineness, near 360—1000ths. Value, $0.176.

No. 511. ***Mexican Half Dollar, Guanaxuato.***

Weight, $"0.496=204.53 grs.=13.25 grms.
Fineness, 896—1000ths. Value, $0.493=2*s.* 0.2*d.*=2.63 fr.

No. 512. ***Mexican Half Dollar, San Luis Potosi.***
Weight, $0.496=204.53 grs.=13.25 grms.
Fineness, 900—1000ths.
Value, $0.496.=2*s*. 0.3*d*.=2.64 fr

CONCLUDING REMARKS.

Soon after entering upon duty as melter and refiner in the New Orleans Mint, in 1839, I became aware that well executed counterfeit Mexican dollars abounded in general circulation to an alarming extent. In trying to devise a remedy for the evil, by rendering their detection easy, I soon conceived an idea of producing something like the foregoing work. The great desideratum in the enterprise, was to print fac-similes of the good and bad coins, that might be relied upon. The method of medal rule engraving, so elegantly exemplified in the excellent and authentic "Manual of Coins and Bullion," by Messrs. Eckfeldt & Dubois, besides being slow and expensive, necessarily obliterates or distorts the more minutely engraven details on the disk of the coin represented, which details are sometimes essential in deciding whether a coin be good or bad. After many trials, overcoming successive difficulties as they presented themselves, I at length succeeded in preparing metal types adapted for printing, indirectly from the coins themselves, which, if they do not always make a handsome print, give a *perfectly* correct, and I think, satisfactory representation. The plan is also applicable to the typographic delineation of medals, cameos, intaglios, and the surface of many objects of natural history: But of all these matters, and the details of the plan itself, I shall give an account at a future time, in a more appropriate place.

In collecting materials for this, and a larger contemplated work, I am under obligations to many persons, very many more than I can here venture to name. It would be ungrateful in me not to express my thanks to J. M. Kennedy, Esq., Superintendent of the New Orleans Mint, for the
25

use of his cabinet of coins; and especially to Dr. Wm. P. Hort, Assayer of the N. O. Mint, for the vast deal of labor he has contributed, in making, at my request, special assays, which it will be observed are given on his authority. To the officers of the Bank of Louisiana, the Mechanics' and Traders' Bank, the State, Gas, and City Banks of New Orleans, I am also greatly indebted. Messrs. Jacob Barker, Col. Daunoy, Wm. E. Leverich, R. M. Davis, Jackson Duplessis, and L. Muh, of New Orleans; and Messrs. Stearns and Davenport, of Boston, have also rendered me especial assistance.

To the courtesy of Dr. R. M. Patterson, Director of the United States Mint, at Philadelphia, and to Messrs. Eckfeldt and Dubois, Assayers, I am indebted for a full suite of the impressions of the rare coins contained in the splendid cabinet of that mint; said impressions having been principally used, however, in preparing types for the larger work above alluded to, and also advertised on the second page.

In preparing the present work, utility has been almost the sole object; hence, explication of the arms, legends, inscriptions, &c., impressed upon the coins, has very seldom been made :—and it will be observed that attention has been given to systematic arrangement only so far as it has promised to subserve the main object proposed.

In conclusion I will add, that I am especially desirous of getting any coins lately issued from foreign mints; and that anything in the way of curious coins or medals, old or new, will be thankfully received and liberally paid for. Persons meeting with counterfeit or doubtful dollars, not contained in this work, by submitting them to me for examination, will not merely confer a personal favor, but will contribute perhaps to discourage the circulation of bad money. Desirous of rendering my general work on modern coins as comprehensive as practicable, I will also be thankful for the temporary loan of curious coins.

INDEX,

REFERRING TO NUMBERS, NOT TO PAGES, UNLESS SO EXPRESSED.

INDEX.

INDEX.

INDEX.